SHEEP
to SHOWBIZ

A Border Collie's Journey from Scotland to America,
and from Herding to Therapy

SHEEP
to SHOWBIZ

Ann Gafke

For information about this title, contact the publisher:

Publisher: Ann Gafke
Publisher website: https://dogschooling.com
Email address: anngafke@dogschoolng.com

ISBNs:
979-8-9920795-0-0 (print)
979-8-9920795-1-7 (eBook)

Printed in the United States of America

Cover and Interior design: 1106 Design

Dedication

To my husband, Roger, the love of my life,
without whom this project would
never have been completed.

TABLE *of* CONTENTS

INTRODUCTION

Dogs are not people in little fur coats, but they have the same emotions as people.

They communicate those emotions differently, of course. While people use verbal language, dogs have very limited verbal language—barks, whines, growls. They use an extensive set of body-language signals. For example, dogs can raise their hair on their neck, back, tail all at once or any part of it by itself. They can wag, tuck, hold their tail rigid to send messages. Also, notice how your dog "talks" to you with their eyes and eyebrows.

My goal in *Sheep to Showbiz* is to help readers learn how to communicate better with their dog—how to "read" their dog, taking into consideration all of the circumstances and the dog's point of view. So, when you say, "I told him/her in plain English . . ." Understand, English is not the dog's natural language. When a dog acts fearful in public, you may "calm" down the dog with soothing petting and a "It's okay, baby . . . you're okay." You think you are encouraging the dog—and you are! You are telling your dog that he or she is right to behave in this way—scared. Instead, give the dog an "Ah, Ah." Tell the dog to get over himself/herself and direct the dog to work . . . sit, down, stand, heel. Then praise when the dog redirects his or her behavior.

In this book, follow Miste through her sometimes sad, sometimes traumatic, sometimes humorous, sometimes serving, and always educational experiences. You will take away an appreciation of a dog's learning, thinking, feeling, and serving. You will increase your knowledge of dog behavior, dog education, and the values of that education.

CHAPTER 1

THE BEGINNING

The June air was softly tinted with the smell of sweet, clean straw and hay. The Wise Old Goat, who, as far as I know, had lived here forever and knew everything, was munching on some grain that Mom Sheena, our human mother, had put into his feed box. I was playing with my brothers and sisters in our 500-year-old stone barn on a Scottish hillside beside the River Tay in Perthshire, Scotland. Well, anyway, that's what the Wise Old Goat told us—that this barn was 500 years old. I suppose he knew, because I'm sure he had been there through all of those years! I really didn't care how old the barn was. All I cared about was sliding through the new straw and burrowing under it to hide from my brother, who was "it."

The sound of a car driving in got our attention, and we all rushed to the gate to see who it was. The boys all started barking. Honestly! They are so irresponsible. We girls wait to see who it is first. It might be a friend, and then how stupid would we look—barking at a friend! A man and a woman got out as Mom Sheena emerged from the house to greet them warmly. See! I was right. They were friends. We had never seen them before, but if Mom Sheena said they were okay, then they were okay, and we should be respectful. . . . But, oh, no, not those upstart, ruffian boys. Mom Sheena chatted for a moment; then she headed straight for us and opened the gate from the barn so we could greet these friends. I ran to the woman, as she had a kind-looking face. She smelled good, too, so I sat on her foot.

It turned out that the man, "Jim," was her husband, and they had come to get acquainted with us to see if they would like to invite one of us to live with them. Our mom, Skye, had told us all about this, saying we would, when it was time, be going out into the world to be on our own with our own families. So. This must be the time. I sized this person up to see if I liked her, as she seemed to be making the decisions. "Grace" and her husband, Jim, looked at each of us. I had listened to my mother, and I had planned ahead of time so that, when the time came, I would decide if I liked that person or not and would act accordingly. I decided I really liked this person. She was gentle and kind. Also, it was obvious she didn't know a lot about dogs. That was affirmed when she told Mom Sheena she had never owned a dog before. Yes! This was the person I wanted! I could train her from the beginning! I could mold her into just the kind of owner I wanted!

I quickly glanced around. None of the other kids were paying attention to the human conversation. They were all showing off. So, they had not heard all this information. As Grace picked up each of the other puppies, he or she squirmed and wiggled to get down to show off more. I sat quietly on Grace's foot the whole time. I wanted this woman for myself. When it came to my time to be picked up and examined, I snuggled in close to Grace. I liked how gentle she was and how delighted she was to be in our company. Yes, this was a human who had great potential, and I liked her very much, so I snuggled even deeper into her arms, sending her mental messages about how I should stay here—that I should be her dog. I gave her little polite kisses, not messy, sloppy ones. I was trying to show her I could be as gentle as she was. Grace pulled me closer to her and looked over the rest of my brothers and sisters. "I want this one," she announced, and she would not put me down.

Grace squeezed me tight and carried me to the house, where we went into the kitchen. I loved that kitchen. It was filled with the most delicious smells, from cheese to fresh-baked bread, soups, and all kinds of delicious smells that I didn't recognize, but they sure smelled good. It was fun, because every time you went in there, the smells were different. The humans all sat down at the big maple table. I was in Grace's lap. The humans started talking about papers and pedigrees. Ours is an old royal family. Our ancestry can be traced to the very beginning of all Collies. That requires a lot of paperwork going through a lot of human organizations. I just snuggled in, reminding Grace she had made the right decision and convincing her I was worth all the trouble of all this paperwork.

I knew I was destined to herd sheep, too, like my Border Collie ancestors. The Wise Old Goat had told us, and so had our mother, Skye. We had spent part of every day watching our father, Moss, herd the sheep. Some days, he had to work all day. My dad was wonderful. He had saved Mom Sheena's house from being burglarized two times. The second time, he held the burglars in the barn until the law arrived. I don't know how he did it, but he just knew who was going to cause trouble and who was a genuinely nice person. He could totally charm anyone or protect his family—human and canine—and the sheep, cattle, chickens, cats, and even the Wise Old Goat. My dad could do just everything. The Wise Old Goat used to tell us stories about him.

One of my favorite stories was how Moss had begun herding sheep. My dad, Moss, was Mom Sheena's father's favorite dog. Moss went everywhere with his master. He didn't herd sheep because he was too busy being a constant companion. Mom Sheena had grown up on the farm and became a nurse for people, but after her husband died, she moved her family back to the farm. When her father died, she inherited the farm. Now, however, she could not handle the sheep by herself. As she thought about how she was going to get help, she said to herself: *After all, Moss is a Collie. He was descended from Border Collies—the breed with the reputation for being the best herding dogs on Earth, and also number one in canine intelligence. Moss certainly ought to be able to herd sheep.* Never mind that he had never been taught anything about herding. Also, never mind that Mom Sheena had no experience in teaching a dog to herd sheep.

Mom Sheena gestured out across the field of sheep and said to Moss, "Bring me the sheep." Moss looked up at her and wagged his tail. He was sure she was talking to him, but he was clueless as to what she was saying. Again, Mom Sheena made the gesture, and again she said to Moss, "Bring me the sheep." Moss now realized she was trying to communicate with him, but what did she want? For the third time, she gestured and said, "Bring me the sheep." Moss stood for a few minutes, looking at Mom Sheena, and then he looked out to the sheep in the pasture. He thought of his master, who had always wanted the sheep around him, and then of Mom Sheena's gestures. Maybe *that's* what she wanted.

He turned and trotted out toward the sheep and started to gather them up. He got them to gather around Mom Sheena, who, unaware of what a feat Moss had accomplished, had moved on to the next task. She needed the sheep in the barn, which was across a moderately busy paved road with no fence on either end because of the road. Then, he needed to get the sheep through the barn door. Somehow, he did it.

There are lots of reasons why sheep need to be put in the barn. The ones we were keeping needed to be marked with paint, so they'd be easier to sort out when the time came for selling the others; that way, we'd still be able to keep them all in the same pasture. The paint made them much easier to sort. All the sheep needed yearly blood draws for various health issues, vaccinations, and on and on. The next morning, Mom Sheena thought, *Well, Moss took them in; maybe he will take them back out.*

Again, Moss did it! From then on, Moss was the farm's herding dog. He became especially valuable during lambing season. When a ewe (that's a girl sheep) has a baby lamb, frequently it scares her (sheep are not very smart), and she will run from it and hide in the rest of the flock. If she is not reunited with her baby within one hour, she will forget she even had a baby and refuse to feed it. The lamb then becomes an orphan and has to be hand-fed every couple of hours, which is difficult for Mom Sheena and not good for the baby lamb. Each lamb has a unique smell, different from any other lamb but identical to his or her mother. Moss became an expert at being able to quickly find the correct mothers in the flock, even when there were multiple lambs involved at the same time. I was proud to be my dad's kid. If I worked very hard, maybe someday I could be as good as he is. I had a lot to learn. . . . *I'll start tomorrow.* Right then, I was busy in the kitchen, working on getting a permanent home.

At last, we walked to the car. It hit me. I was not being taken back to the barn but to the car with Grace and her husband. I had one last scare. They put me down in the grass. Had they changed their minds? Were they leaving me here? The grass tickled my tummy. I suddenly *had* to go potty. So, I did. Grace immediately began telling me what a good girl I was. *Really? I do that all the time. Won't they be happy!*

Grace picked me up again, holding me close, and we got into the car.

I had ridden in a car once before . . . well, actually, it was a truck . . . from the farm to a place Mom Sheena called "the vet." We were put on a table, and the man poked and prodded me, looking into my stomach through my mouth! I thought he poked his fingers into places I thought were entirely inappropriate. I found out he was called "the vet," and he proceeded to stick me with sticky things that hurt. I heard him call those things "shots." I would have to remember that as a bad word.

Now, I wondered if they were going to "the vet." Maybe I should be sorry I had pushed to get chosen. But we did not arrive at "the vet." We got out at a house. I wondered how these humans knew where to go. Did they just decide this was a good place to stop?

There were lots of houses all around. You could hear lots of other cars and trucks, dogs, and children. But we went in. Once we went in, I knew they lived here. Their scent was all over the place. This was their den . . . well, house. Grace put me down on a very shiny and slippery surface, which was a little scary, because my feet kept sliding out from under me. I was so embarrassed and made a note to work hard on how to walk on these floors. The house was called Oak Grove Cottage at Leith. My new home was also the home of this wonderful woman.

I learned a lot in the next few weeks. I learned that, even though the legs of those things they called "tables" and "chairs" *look* like sticks, they are not to be played with or chewed on. In fact, nothing in the house was to be chewed on or played with, except a few things the humans called "Miste's toys." That is my new name. The "Mi" came from Grace's son, named Mitchel, and the "ste" came from her daughter's name, Stephanie. Well, I have *also* got one of those fancy names. It is Gaell of Finlaggan. Don't laugh. Remember, please, these people were honoring me with a name they felt showed the dignity of all those generations of purebred Collies before me. No one ever calls me by that name, and they did give me a lovely name—"Miste"—and everyone calls me that, and that is what counts. I am sure many of you have names you don't get called by, either. *Charles* becomes "Chuck," or "Chas," or "Charlie." *Richard* becomes "Rich," or "Dick," or "Ricky." You get the idea.

I learned I could not sleep on chairs or the big, soft couch. I had to sit by the door and get my feet cleaned before I could walk further into the house. I learned Grace was not well. Sometimes she had to sit down from our play to rest. When that happened, I would run to my rest spot on the hearth of the fireplace and lie down to wait until Grace's rest was over and it was time to play again.

There were lots of things to learn, but none of them was about the sheep and how to get them going in the direction you wanted them to go. And where was the barn with its clean, swishy straw? Where were the pastures where you could look clear to the River

Tay and watch the sheep grazing in small families dotted over the pasture? I missed my brothers, sisters, and my mother, Skye, and dad, Moss. I missed the Wise Old Goat, who used to tell us stories about our parents, grandparents, and their lives on the farm.

However, there was Grace. What a joy! Grace spent a lot of time with me. She taught me lots of things, and I learned to understand every word she said to me. Sometimes, we just sat together, and she would read to me. She loved the *Harry Potter* series. I could tell when she was happy, sad, worried, or not feeling well. We went on walks and met other dogs, children, all kinds of different people, and all sorts of things. Sometimes, she took me with her when she went to Edinburgh. We would walk on the crowded streets or through the park near the Scott Memorial, where the Ferris wheel is. There was so much to do there.

I was four months old then. Grace had never had a dog before. She needed help. Grace had a sister, Hanna, who lived with her husband, Alec, in Dunkeld, Scotland. Grace had heard that her sister knew an American couple visiting Scotland who had a dog school in America. Grace asked her sister to ask the Americans to help her with her new puppy. So, when the Americans came to Scotland at the end of July, they visited with Grace and me. I didn't know where the United States was, but the prospect of a visit surely sounded important. I was told to be on my best behavior. I was lying on the grass outside when they arrived; I pretended not to pay attention, but I kept my eye on them, sizing up these new people. So, when they came into the house, I took my place at the hearth and waited for a chance to play with these people, who talked with an accent I had never heard. I also wondered what a *dog school* was. I discovered I liked these Americans and their granddaughter. They obviously liked me, too. It was the first time

I had seen the lady I have come to know as "Auntie Ann," the man I now call "Uncle Roger," and my kid, "Lauren."

The Americans laid out a schooling plan for me. Then they were gone. Little did I know then that, within six months, I would move to their home in the United States. Little did I know the United States was soooo far away!

In August, I could tell Grace was having more days of not feeling well. The talk got heavier; there was no laughter. I tried to let Grace know I was there for her. It got worse. I heard Grace talking to people on the phone and to people who visited the house. Some were saying they wanted me. Some were saying they would take me if I didn't have any place to go. *What was going on here? Had I disappointed them somehow? Just tell me, and I will fix it.* I didn't want to move. I wanted to stay here. Why couldn't I just stay here with Grace? I loved Grace. I knew she loved me, too. What was going on here? Everyone got quieter, and I could not make anything out except the gloom and depression.

One day, Grace did not come home from her doctor's appointment. The days became long and lonely. I grieved for Grace. Jim did not spend much time at home. He would let me out to go potty. He fed me. Otherwise, I was alone, mostly left in my crate. I missed Grace. I felt as if my heart was about to break. Frequently, I broke into long howls of utter despair. I didn't know where Grace was or what was happening to her without me to watch over her. I knew the family was busy, but there was nothing I could do but lie in the gloom of my crate. Then, on Christmas Day, Jim came home with Mitchel and Stephanie. Grace had died. I felt like I had died, too.

The next week was a blur. I didn't care. Nothing mattered, because Grace was gone. I found out that the American couple were going to take me to America. I didn't care. It didn't matter.

Nothing mattered anymore. I was taken to "the vet," where he poked and prodded again, took my temperature, and gave me some more sticky things. Alec filled out a bunch of paperwork. I didn't care.

Then, the day before New Year's Eve, I was taken to Grace's sister's house, where we met the American man named "Roger," the man I would come to know as "Uncle Roger."

CHAPTER 2

WHAT I DIDN'T KNOW

Although I didn't know it at the time, and, even if I had, I would not have cared, because all I could think about was Grace and how I longed to hear her voice again. I didn't know that the Americans had a dog school in America and an excellent line of German Shepherd Dogs. This line included many Champions[1], top obedience dogs, Register of Merit[2] dogs, dogs serving as guide dogs for the blind, undercover drug-detection dogs[3], therapy dogs, who visit hospitals, nursing homes, schools, and courtrooms to help children testify more comfortably. The line was also a very strong line of OFA[4] hip-and-elbow-certified dogs.

---

1 See Miste's Vocabulary—Chapter 22
2 See Miste's Vocabulary—Chapter 22
3 See Miste's Vocabulary—Chapter 22
4 See Miste's Vocabulary—Chapter 22

The Americans were very careful about where they placed their puppies. They wanted them placed where they would be educated and useful.

One of these puppies was placed with a policewoman named "Barbara" who named the puppy "Roger & Out" and made him her partner—they were an undercover drug-detection team[5]. They had many successes and arrests. They were so successful that Roger & Out had a contract out on him from the underworld. That meant that whoever killed this dog would get money.

One day, the flu overcame Barbara, and she had to go to the pharmacy to get a prescription. She felt lousy as she trudged across the mall toward the pharmacy, with Roger & Out by her side. All she could think about was breathing and recovering from the constant barrage of coughing. Barbara did not notice Roger & Out alert on a man standing in front of a store window. The man was a drug dealer, and he noticed when Roger & Out alerted on him[6]. He recognized that Roger & Out was an undercover drug-detection dog[7], and if that was true, then Barbara was the police. He let her pass. Barbara got her prescription and started to retrace her steps back across the mall.

The man had disappeared from the storefront, but as Barbara and her canine partner approached a lamppost fifty feet farther down the mall, Roger & Out growled, his body stiffened, and the hair on his neck and back flashed up; he let out a chilling, snarling growl as the drug dealer stepped from behind the post and started shooting at Barbara and Roger & Out. Barbara rolled sideways as Roger & Out leapt forward toward the drug dealer, crossing

---

5 See Miste's Vocabulary—Chapter 22
6 See Miste's Vocabulary—Chapter 22
7 See Miste's Vocabulary—Chapter 22

the distance and instantly engaging the man in a fight. Barbara called for backup.

Roger & Out fought with the drug dealer, knocking the gun out of his hand. When the police backup arrived, Roger & Out had the drug dealer disarmed and pinned to the ground. The police took custody of the drug dealer. Barbara ran to Roger & Out's side and threw her arms around his neck to hug him. He collapsed in her arms, and that was when she discovered he had been shot. He had been mortally wounded. He was dying. In another minute, the great dog was gone. He had saved his owner's, handler's—his partner's—life. He had carried out his duty as a police officer. He was a hero. That is the kind of bloodline I was moving into, but I was too lost in grief to care about things like that.

Also, there was something I didn't know then but have since come to appreciate—this family's Scottish connections. The American woman's great-uncle Charlie owned a business in Scotland renting out Border Collies and herdsmen to move sheep for lambing, shots, shearing, or to new grazing grounds. Charlie had come to the U.S. and had brought a Border Collie, Jean, who, while she was being shipped to America, whelped (that means "gave birth to") a litter of puppies in the Kansas City train depot on a Sunday morning. Her picture with the puppies appeared on the front page of the *Kansas City Star* newspaper.

There were requests from all over the country for one of those puppies. The American woman was given one of those puppies. However, the puppy needed to live at the American woman's grandparents' house. "Lassie," as the puppy was named, got bored at the house. There was no work to do, and the fence was only four feet tall, so she jumped the fence and went on walkabouts to keep herself entertained. Unfortunately, there were two major highways close by, and the American woman's grandparents were afraid Lassie would be hit and killed. All of this was taking place during World War II.

One day, an Army man was visiting the farm, and he fell in love with Lassie. The farm was Sni-A-Bar Farms. It was in a trust to be operated as an agricultural experiment station for 30 years after the death of William Rockhill Nelson, owner of the *Kansas City Star* newspaper. The United States Department of Agriculture operated the experiment station on the farms. The farms had a steady stream of distinguished visitors, both foreign and domestic.

The farms also had a show herd of Shorthorn cattle that was known over most of the world. Auntie Ann's grandfather was manager of the farms. He judged Shorthorns in all the major shows in this country and in many other countries around the world. He is in the Shorthorn Hall of Fame.

The Army man said he wanted her for the Army. He said she would never be sent to the front but would be used instead to train other dogs. Although she was just a child, the American woman understood. She didn't want Lassie to be hit by a car, either. She understood that Lassie would be bored and not stay inside the fence. The American woman's own father was in the service, so she understood how everyone needed to do everything they could do for the war. So, Lassie went to the Army. She trained many dogs who would be sent into battle. Lassie herself never went to either the European theatre of the war or the South Pacific theatre but continued to train other dogs. She was excellent with this assignment. After the war, she continued to live with the young Army officer who had met her at the farm. She had a litter of puppies, and he sent a grandson of her's back to the farm. They named the puppy "Jock."

The Americans and their grandchildren, Lauren and Amanda, had been visiting Scotland for several years by that time. They had found their family roots and had made Scottish friends. So now, even though they had an outstanding bloodline of German Shepherd Dogs, the thought of getting a Border Collie was fun. After all, could there be a better souvenir of Scotland than a live Border Collie—Scotland's number-one working dog?

I didn't know any of that. All I knew was that I had been taken to Grace's sister's house in Dunkeld, Scotland. This was a sad time. I learned that the Americans had offered to take me to their home and that Grace herself wanted that move. I didn't care. Grace was gone. Nothing mattered, but Grace wanted this, so I would do it for her.

Dunkeld has flowers in the summer and snow in the winter. At Dunkeld, there is a bridge over the River Tay to drive over when you go into the village. The River Tay is one of seven major salmon rivers in Scotland. Near the bridge, there is a beautiful riverside park with ducks! When Grace made one of her many trips to visit Hanna, her sister, I always longed to herd those ducks! I heard the American woman liked to feed the ducks. Humm. That is interesting—she likes ducks, too. There is also a beautiful old cathedral there. The minister is in my extended human family. I found out the American man and woman attended services there on their wedding anniversary. Interesting. The cathedral is very old. Early Scotsmen started building it more than seven hundred years ago. I have no idea how long that is, do you? The Wise Old Goat just said none of us had even been born then. Weird.

There is also a Beatrix Potter Park there. Beatrix Potter spent summers there and wrote stories about Peter Rabbit and his sisters, Flopsy, Mopsy, and Cottontail. I would love to chase rabbits. Oh!

No! Never *hurt* them—just *chase* them. I think you call it "playing tag." Rabbits are really fast. I can be fast, too. I wonder if they have rabbits in America. Not that it mattered—nothing really mattered then. I just wondered. I have no idea who Beatrix Potter is, but I am sure the Wise Old Goat had met her. It was winter then in Dunkeld, and there was lots of snow on the ground.

The view out of Hanna and Alec's front door is a large field with sheep. *I bet I would be good at herding sheep—just like my father!* As we arrived at Alec and Hanna's house, I watched the sheep, dotted over a large, beautiful landscape of snow. The sheep were all toasty, warm, and cozy in their winter-wool fleece coats. On previous visits, I had found and played with pheasants, grouse, deer, and other animals at Hanna's and Alec's house lots of times. I have to say, I haven't had much success. They don't seem to catch on to the game of it. They are supposed to run away or fly up and come right back, but they don't. They fly away and don't come back for hours. Still, one can be hopeful. Alec and Hanna frequently have deer that come right up to their front window. That window looks out over a fenced grazing field that frequently has not only sheep in it but also a small herd of deer nearby.

Dunkeld is a village of about 500 people and attracts lots and lots of tourists. There are many interesting shops and things to do, including a "Going Potty" shop, where you paint ceramic things. The American family painted ceramic things every year. I walked past that shop often. I was never allowed to go in—something about a *bull in a china shop.* I know about sheep, but I've never met a bull.

Tomorrow at 10 a.m., the American man, Alec, and I will start the hour-long drive to Edinburgh to catch the train to London from Waverley Station to King's Cross Station in London. Alec and Hanna are in Edinburgh today to meet the American man.

It is snowing, and it is supposed to be snowing tomorrow. I don't care, but I wonder why these people do.

Weeks later, the American woman described a call from Hanna when they met the American man at Haymarket Station in Edinburgh. The American woman reported in an email to family members about the American man's trip to bring me to America:

"A crackly voice with lots of noise of loudspeakers announcing the arrival and departure of trains from the bustling train station said a cheery 'Hello' and 'Just a minute . . .' and then Hanna's Scottish-accented voice came on, and she said, 'Your husband is just an angel!' I said, 'I know that; that's why I married him!'"

Hanna said the end came quickly for Grace, her sister, Miste's human mom. Hanna also said that Grace was very happy that we were taking Miste because we were just the home she would want for her. Hanna said Grace loved Miste very much and that Grace was so relieved that we were taking Miste, because she knew that was where she wanted her to be the most. It made me feel very humble and grateful that we could bring Grace that kind of comfort.

They were speaking from Haymarket Station in Edinburgh. Edinburgh is such a fascinating city. The architecture is sandstone, or most of it is. Because sandstone is soft, it can be sculpted more easily than granite, which is the primary stone for some other Scotland cities, like Aberdeen. Edinburgh is the capital of Scotland. It is a large city but a surprisingly warm and informal one. The people are friendly and very nice—the Americans had been there more than once. Haymarket is just beyond downtown. It is where the farmers used to come with all their wares and livestock and harvest. It's about two or three miles from the end of the train line at Waverley Station. Haymarket is just below Edinburgh Castle, just off Princes Street (and yes, it is Princes Street, not Princess

Street). The Haymarket is not very far from the old Bakers District, either. That is where the grist mills would grind the grain, and the bakeries would bake all the bread for the city; each morning, the vendors picked it up and distributed it around the city.

I, Miste, didn't know then that the American woman had painted a picture of the Bakers District of the little river, The Water of Leith, from a picture in a book. I would see her painting in America when I moved there. The American woman looked for that location on her trips to Edinburgh and found it.

Alec and Hanna have gone to meet the American man at Haymarket to take him to their home in Dunkeld. The snow was deep at Alec and Hanna's house. I watched the sheep in the snowy pastures. I saw a pheasant hunting for seeds and a couple of rabbits playing and rolling in the snow. For a moment, the despair lifted, and a kind of peace settled over me. The American will sleep here tonight, and we will become acquainted in this storybook place with storybook scenery.

It was snowing the next morning when Alec drove us from Dunkeld to the train station in Edinburgh to start our journey to America. The American man reported to his wife about the progress of his trip. Here is what he wrote about our journey from Dunkeld to London: "Early successes—relieved herself on lead twice this morning (he is writing about me). First leg uneventful, leaving snowy (18 inches) Dunkeld for the Waverley train station in Edinburgh by car. In Edinburgh, the City Center streets are blocked off for the New Year's Eve celebration for most of the week (like Times Square)."

We—Alec, the American, and I (Miste)—arrived in Edinburgh, and Alec drove around a while. The streets around the train depot at Waverley Station had all been closed off because of the Scottish

New Year celebration, called Hogmanay[8] (pronounced: Hog-ma-nay). That meant the American had to wheel me in my crate for blocks and blocks down the center of Edinburgh, down Princes Street to Waverley Station below the Castle, from the Caledonian Hotel, which is an old train station and has the most interesting interior architecture. We passed the Overseas Press Club, where he and the American woman had stood on the roof last year to watch the Hogmanay fireworks over the castle and along Princes Street. We passed the museum, where this man, his wife, and his grandchild saw the Andy Warhol exhibit. Then we passed the castle, where the Americans came to see the Tattoo each year; we passed Jenner's (the oldest department store in Scotland); we passed the impressive Scott Monument, and proceeded almost to the Balmoral Hotel, where J.K. Rowling wrote the final chapters of the *Harry Potter* series.

This American man wheeled me, and it was kind of like I was going where I had been and where we, this American man and I, have now been together, and, now, I was becoming part of it all. It was a funny kind of feeling. Maybe there was more to these people than I thought. But probably not.

The American man wrote more:

"Second leg (glad there are no photos except for the hundreds of UK security pictures of this leg).

"Down the street, the old man walked in blustery winds with some slushy ice on the sidewalks, dog crate tethered with bungee cords to a set of old luggage wheels, and a travel case, stopping only when the crate tumbled over from the uneven sidewalk or slush.

---

8 See Miste's Vocabulary—Chapter 22

"Third leg underway is a four-hour and forty-minute train ride to King's Cross Station in London. Then, I suspect, a repeat of Leg 2, when we get to London.

"Train is great. Miste is beside me in her crate. We can ride all the way in this manner unless a person who uses a wheelchair gets on at one of the stops. Then we have to do something (unspecified at this point) else." He ended the email.

Well, the train may have been great for him, but not for me. The train terminal—where the trains were, was a huge building. It echoed and had very loud speakers blaring out. It was enough to scare you out of your wits. There were people everywhere, many of them hurrying here and there. Some were sitting on benches around the area. It appeared to be like outside, but inside at the same time. The air was outside air, but the terminal was filled with all sorts of smells: food, people, suitcases, bags with who knows what inside them.

There were pigeons flying everywhere and landing on the pavement, hunting for crumbs that people would drop from the food they were eating. Who could even think about eating in this place? Some of the shops were open stalls, and some of the shops were closed in with doors and windows. There were signs everywhere. Some would flash. Some were lit, and some of them were just big signs hanging there. So many voices . . . which ones were you supposed to listen to? Some of them were children's voices, some excited, some tired, and some crying. Other voices were women's, and some were men's. Some were rushed, some drawling, and, once in a while, they had an angry tone. We jostled along. I was glad to be in my crate. It sort of hid me from all the noise. Still, it was upsetting. I had never been in a place like this before. This was so different from the long, silent hours I had spent in my crate at

Grace's house. I was nervous, and I whimpered—just in case the American could make all this better.

At last, a man helped the American hoist my crate onto the train, and I was placed in a corner, sort of under a table. The American threw his coat over part of the crate that stuck out from under the table and sat down beside me on the other side. I felt safer now with this man. He was calm and definitely knew what he was doing. But what were we doing here? I had never traveled by train before. Why couldn't we go by car? Why had we said goodbye to Alec? Grace had wanted me to do this, so there was nothing left but to watch and try to process all that was happening. Well, at least, I had my crate around me, and this American man seemed to know what we were doing here. This certainly was not like anything I'd ever experienced.

I need to report one situation on the train trip that the American man described as "unusual" when he talked with his wife in America, but I didn't think it was anything out of the ordinary. It's what I was born to do. We were located at the end of one of the cars, quite near the loo (that's what Scottish people call the restroom.), so folks passed by frequently. I was quiet for the first couple of hours, despite all the strangers passing by, until my senses alerted me to one man, walking slowly down the aisle, stopping every now and then. He worried me. I sensed a hostility in him. I barked to alert the American. *Arrrf! Arrrf!* When the man stopped at the row where we were sitting, this man, in a gruff, mean voice, demanded, "What's that dog doing here? *He* (referring to me . . . who is a girl) ought to be in the baggage car." The American replied that the man's colleague in Edinburgh had told us to sit here. The man grunted and walked on. I learned he was *the conductor*. I think I was right to have alerted the American. I was quiet again for the rest of the trip.

I was glad I was there. Maybe this man needed me more than I originally thought. Maybe I'd better start paying more attention to my job and figure out how I can help more.

We got to London with nothing else to report beyond the run-in with the grouchy conductor. We got off the train at King's Cross Station—the station in the *Harry Potter* stories. We didn't have much time to look for Platform 9 & 3/4s, however. We loaded all of our stuff into one of London's famous black taxis for the trip across town to the Airport Hotel Hilton. The taxi looked like a car to me, but my crate and all of our stuff fit in it. Sometimes we can't fit in a car. So, maybe that is the difference—the size. It was 4:30 p.m., and it was almost totally dark already. The American was surprised. He'd forgotten that Scotland is short on daylight in the winter and long on daylight in the summer. In the summer, it is light from 4 a.m. to around 10 p.m., but in the winter, it gets dark by 4:15 p.m.

We walked into the hotel. I had never been in a hotel before. It was a huge building, all very streamlined, all glass, and very shiny floors. I sure was glad I had learned to walk on shiny floors. There were people all over. Everyone looked like they were in a hurry to get to somewhere important. My American got a ground-floor room so that he could take me outside to potty on the large grassy area, but, are you kidding? No way was I going to do such a private thing in this strange place. My American gave up, and as he was taking me back into the building, he threw two pieces of these dog treats into some bushes beside the steps. I pretended not to notice. I needed to think about it. How could he throw those treats away? They were really, really good treats. Just because I hadn't gone to potty, he didn't need to throw them away! What a waste, and I am Scottish. We don't waste anything!

Ninety minutes later, he took me out again. I knew what I was going to do. I headed straight for those bushes and retrieved those two small pieces of those very, very good dog treats. This American seemed surprised that I remembered them or even noticed them. *Of course, I noticed. Does he think I'm stupid or something?*

We stayed overnight there. In the morning, I pooped twice. Yes, I had figured out that, if I pooped or piddled, I got those delicious dog treats, and there was no more throwing them in the bushes to just go to waste. My travel companion gave me only very small sips of water through the night so that I would not have to potty in my crate on the plane. In the morning, he gave me some honey for energy—but not dog food, so I wouldn't have to poop on the long trip. He also gave me a raw potato to chew on if I got thirsty or bored—and lots of newspapers, just in case. Who could get bored with all this stuff going on? He also gave me some ice cubes in my crate pan so that I could whet my whistle on them. My head didn't know what to look at first! It was New Year's Eve morning now. We headed for Heathrow Airport.

When we got to the airport, we had to go through this thing called "security." They patted everyone down and ran this scanner over them. I had to go through an X-ray machine, where they could see my innards. Evidently, I was normal. I discovered I was riding with two Border Collie puppies from Wales. They appeared to be eight or nine weeks old. If *they* weren't scared, I sure wasn't going to get shown up, so neither was I. After all, I had lived through a train and a hotel, so get on with it.

It was important to get on the airplane before the temperature in Dallas, Texas, or Kansas City, Missouri, dropped to -12 degrees Celsius. Americans use a different scale, called "Fahrenheit." On that scale, the minimum would be 10 degrees. If it is that cold, dogs can't fly. The temperature was headed in that direction in both cities. Once you are on the plane, the journey must be completed. The airplane is heated. They just worry about dogs in crates sitting on the tarmac in the extreme cold. Our flight was a go. I was in my crate in the plane, and I thought we were off to America. But now, besides temperatures to worry about, there were crates in strange places and, on this, my first flight, the plane was delayed for security reasons. What did that mean? Of course, no one considers telling a "dog" much. We have to pick up whatever information we can catch on our own.

Now I was wondering where the American man was. Was he okay? I felt like he would know what to do. I would be safe with him, and he would be safe with me protecting him against grouchy conductors and such. We needed to be together. After what seemed like forever, I guess the temperatures were okay and the "Security" issues had been resolved, because we were taking off for a new home in America for me. Wow!

CHAPTER 3

JOURNEY TO AMERICA

The flight was sooo looooong. I finally succumbed to the drone of the engines and the warmth and fell asleep. We were in the air for 10 hours. I slept a lot and chewed on my potato. The ice cubes were gone, but the potato was fine. When we landed in Dallas, I was glad, I had to admit, to see the American man. It was comforting to know we were still together on this strange journey. In the air, on the long flight, I had decided I would call the American man "Uncle Roger." We were on this journey together, and I was supposed to go to live with him. It just seemed more fitting.

In Dallas, we had another scare. The temperature had dropped to below zero in Kansas City, which was where we were going. Uncle Roger *did* have a backup plan. He would make hotel reservations in Dallas if they wouldn't let us on the Kansas City flight. Then, he would rent a car and drive to Kansas City if he had to. Uncle Roger was pretty smart! I liked this man. However, as it turned out, there was an airline rule that, once you had started on your journey, you had to continue on it to the end. We were good to go.

Uncle Roger had to pick me up in Dallas, walk through Customs and Security, and get me onto another plane to Kansas City. Once more, I had to go through the X-ray machine. Honestly, I have had these innards for all my life, and they have never changed, so I don't see why they think they would change now in just a few hours. Oh, well. I'm learning that sometimes these humans are not the brightest creatures on Earth—except for my Uncle Roger! We were put on a plane again. How long *was* this trip, anyway? What was at the end of all this?

Uncle Roger said he planned to be sleeping a lot so that he would be ready for whatever might lie ahead. Once again, I finally succumbed to the drone of the engines. By the time we got to Kansas City, the temperature had fallen to -18 degrees Celsius, which is below zero in American Fahrenheit, but no mind. It was midnight—a new year and a new home for me! Wow!

At this time, I had no idea the American woman had driven three hours to get to the airport in Kansas City and was pacing a path on the floor in the waiting room there. Uncle Roger was the first one off the plane, and he found the American woman I would come to know as "Auntie Ann." Then they waited and waited and waited for me. Finally, Uncle Roger left his luggage with the American woman and went to find me. She was beginning to really worry. She wrote this in a note back to Hanna and Alec:

"I saw a black-and-white dog with a plumy black tail pulling Roger across the terminal. She was a little hesitant coming up to me at first, but when she got a good whiff, she seemed to decide that I probably wasn't that bad. I took her leash, and Roger took the luggage. She was curious about the people she saw and went to greet several (good sign), but she had trepidations about some of them who seemed pushy. She had no qualms about the elevators or automatic doors, although she had never seen any of them before. We put the crate in the back of the car; she was going to ride between my feet in the front seat, and Roger was going to drive. However, it didn't take her but a few minutes to hop and climb into my lap, where she curled up and watched out the windows with interest and then curled in tighter to me. . . . I was massaging her, of course . . . and she went to sleep.

"We made two pit stops for her on the way home. We got home at 3 a.m. She wasn't really happy about going into the crate upstairs by the bed, but when the lights went out, she settled in and slept for the three hours that were left in the night. How much fun it is to have a dog as a 'First Footer.'"[9]

In Scotland, a "First Footer" is the special distinction of the first visitor to your house in the new year. The First Footer is to bring a gift to the household, usually coal. The First Footer represents good luck for the new year. Miste was the First Footer in her new family's house. Miste did not bring coal; she brought herself. That would bring us all luck."

Now, as I recall, we arrived at this house I had never seen before in the dark. What time was it? It *felt* like about 9 o'clock in the morning. It was dark, but the days in the winter in Scotland were much shorter, and it certainly was cold here, even if there was no snow—just bitterly cold. It **was** 9 a.m.—*in Scotland*. I was right, only here it was 3 a.m., the middle of the night. Scotland is six hours ahead of this place. It wasn't cold enough to ruin my nose.

---

9 See Miste's Vocabulary—Chapter 22

There were dogs here. They must live here because they didn't even bark when we drove up. They must have known who it was.

It's true—I did *not* want to go into a strange crate or even the airline crate. I had been in crates long enough. I was tired. I didn't want to fly anywhere. Finally, Uncle Roger convinced me that the new crate was much bigger and was right beside his bed—which was also the bed of the woman I would soon come to call "Auntie Ann." I was too tired now. I plopped down in the crate. I was near Uncle Roger. I would be safe. In the morning, we would face things; right now, I needed to sleep.

As I remember it, when I woke up, I was not quite sure where I was. Gradually, all the smells started filtering into my brain. There were other dogs here. There were interesting food smells, water, and other people. The sounds were there as well. It sounded like a radio, with a man I did not recognize talking. Someone was muttering in front of a computer. Clinking sounds were coming from somewhere else in the house. They sounded like kitchen sounds to me. Then there were sounds of footsteps, and the woman I had met in Scotland was opening my crate door and coaxing me out, slipping a leash over my head, and taking me to a grassy yard outside. I had to go. I got soft praise: "That was nice."

There was already breakfast in my crate when we got back. I had not eaten since we were in London, so I ate it. As I ate, I heard the conversations of other dogs. They were happy conversations. There was no gloom, no sadness. I can't say I missed my home. I had been miserable there for months, because the rest of the humans were absorbed in taking care of Grace. I understood, but it didn't help my misery and loneliness. I did miss Grace, but I had missed her for months. I understood; I was never going to see her again, but that did not take way the misery and loneness I felt. I sighed.

I curled up to put in another long day filled with loneliness, with nothing to think about except how much I missed Grace and how awful this loneliness was.

I was just curling up to sink into the abyss of gloom when the crate door opened. Surprised, because I had been so absorbed in miserable thoughts, I had not heard her approach. It was the woman I had met in Scotland and in whose lap I had ridden in last night. She opened the crate door, and I was allowed to roam the house. My goodness! There were three people here, and they were all over the house. Keeping track of them would take some getting used to. The three people whom I concluded lived here were Uncle Roger, the American woman I had met in Scotland, and a woman named "Marcia," who was Uncle Roger's and the American woman's daughter. I decided to call the American woman "Auntie Ann" and the woman, Marcia, "Auntie Marcia," since she was in the family. She seemed to know a lot about teaching dogs, and she liked me a lot. She gave me very good treats. They were stuff I had never had before, but they sure were good. They were often very different, but always interesting. It was fun wondering what surprise you were going to get next.

Auntie Marcia was one of the three main teachers here. There were Auntie Ann, Uncle Roger, and Auntie Marcia. Auntie Marcia also usually did most of the nail clipping and tooth-tartar scraping, but I didn't know that at the time. I didn't even know what "nail clipping" and "tooth-tartar scraping" were. I did not like the sound of either of those, but I did learn that I just had to put up with them. I had no other choice.

I was told by Rayne, whom I also didn't know at the time I first came here, that it's like when humans go to the dentist. I was *sure* that "going to the dentist"—whatever *that* is—was easier than getting your tartar scraped and your toenails clipped. It *had* to be. Rayne is a German Shepherd Dog that I met the first day I was here. Rayne had been born here. She sure knows a lot. But I'm getting way ahead of myself.

After a while, the American woman slipped the leash over my head. *Now what?* I wondered. We went to the car, and she put me in. Was our journey not finished yet? Where was Uncle Roger? However, we drove only a short distance, like next door. We got out of the car and entered a tan metal building that didn't look like much from the outside. It certainly didn't look like the stone buildings of my native Scotland! These looked puny and frail—and so *temporary*. Then, I stepped into the building, and *wow*! The whole thing hit me! First, there were the smells of so many different dogs and people that I couldn't even register all of them.

Then, I looked around and saw all sorts of strange things! It took my breath away! The woman walked with me as I went over them (with my *nose* . . . not my feet). The woman explained to me what they were. There was a sway bridge, a swing plank, a tire jump, a window jump, a collapsed tunnel, weave poles, teeter-totter, crawl tunnel, all sorts of bar jumps, high jumps, and broad jumps, a ladder, a dog walk, an A-frame, a table—my head was spinning. She told me I would be walking over, under, and through these things. There was so much stuff here for dogs to do. *I got it! This was a dog school!*

This woman sat down in a chair, took my face in her hands, and began talking to me. "I'm not your Mom Sheena, and I'm not your Mom Grace, but I could be your Auntie Ann, and we could work together." She popped some stuff from her pocket. I had never smelled it before, but it sure smelled good. Auntie Ann broke off a piece of it and offered it to me to eat. I gingerly took it, and *pow*! The flavor hit my tongue, and the scent hit my nose all at the same time. It was so powerful it made me wrinkle my nose and made my mouth ache because it was so good.

Auntie Ann said, "Sit." I did, and she immediately gave me another piece of that delicious stuff she called "string cheese." It didn't take me long to learn when I did what she said to do, I got a piece of that wonderful treat. All too soon, it seemed to me, because I wanted more string cheese, Auntie Ann gave me a pat on the side and said, "That's it" and explained we had just had our first lesson. F-i-r-s-t lesson? I remembered that Grace and Auntie Ann had talked about "lesson plans," but that was when I was just a little kid, and besides, Grace had gotten sick, so we just had a few of those.

I soon found out what "lessons" were. They took place every day, in addition to classes in the training building. I had classes in obedience, freestyle dancing, tricks, agility, drill team, therapy work, and more. My head was overflowing with information. I got up in the morning and, after a full schedule, fell into bed at night exhausted, knowing I had to sleep quickly so that I could work the next day. I found the work interesting and very challenging. Who had time to be gloomy? Who had time to be miserable? I missed Grace, but Auntie Ann said we should take action and make Grace proud of us. So, I just worked harder.

I also got to meet and play with some of my new friends for the first time both canine and human. There were Rusty and Rosie and their person, Elizabeth. Rusty and Rosie are Australian Cattle Dogs. I'm a Border Collie. Lassie, her owner is Charlene, is an Old-Time Scotch Collie. Ace, and his owner, Camryn, were there. Ace is a Pyrenean Shepherd. Ace is really smart. He has more national titles than anyone else here. I met four German

Shepherd Dogs, Axel and Maggie, who belong to Whitney, and Ellie and Quinn who go with Victoria. We are all herding dogs, but we all do it differently. I will be broadening my education and so will they.

Then there are a wide variety of others. Purebred dogs are divided into groups—sporting, hound, working, terrier, non-sporting, toy and herding. There are mixed breed dogs. Some have picked up names like Goldendoodles, Labradoodles, and like Sammy who is a Shih Poo, a combination of Poodle and Shih Tzu. Sammy lives with Laurel. Laurel runs our music on Drill Team. Then there is the genuine All-American. They have lots of breeds in them. Sometimes, you would never be able to guess which breeds. People look for different characteristics in dogs depending on different wants and needs. There is a dog out there for every person's desires. Also, there was Sparkle with Shay, and Reuben and EmmyLu with Kassidy. All three dogs are Jack Russell Terriers. Sparkle is an actress who does her own show at Easter. Reuben pulls a cart and can do all sorts of tricks, and EmmyLu has more therapy visits than anyone on the team. George and Ginger, Bull Terriers, lives with human, Beth. Waggles, a fun, little, very independent Boston Terrier, lives with a Doberman Pincher named Eddie and a Labrador Retriever named Kelsey and their people, Gail and Larry. Then, there's Trooper, an All American who goes with Meridith. He only has three legs, but he can run and play as well as anyone. He has such a wonderful temperament. He's in great demand as a therapy dog. Stella Pink who belongs to Debbie, is a happy, independent bully-breed mix who is very sweet, happy, fun-loving, and who loves to talk. I'd never met so many other dogs in my life that were so different from me.

We had our first picture taken as a new family. *I'm* the one who's different. The rest were all German Shepherd Dogs. I had never met a German Shepherd Dog before, but I have learned they love to play, just like me. I heard Auntie Ann and Auntie Marcia say how good I was at play. I was surprised they would have thought otherwise. "Play" could be my middle name. As one of our friends would later say, "Miste is a full-time party animal."

I learned I was now living in Columbia, Missouri, USA. It is a l-o-n-g way from Dunkeld, Scotland. I am trying to learn American English. They sure do talk differently here. I have a hard time understanding them sometimes. The food here is good. I have gained a little weight, but not much. You get to run a lot here. I have a job. I run the legs off of four German Shepherd Dogs. I would like to complain about having to work, but I just can't *because it's so much fun.* They chase me, and I herd them. One of them jumped clear over my back as we were running and fell into a somersault. I thought she had broken her neck, but noooo, she was up and runnin' again.

We also go to school six days a week. There are even more practices on top of that. When I come home, I'm ready for bed. Auntie Ann laughs at the way I sleep. I don't think it's that funny, but she does. I just roll over and go to sleep, so that I'm ready to guard the door in the morning.

In the morning, we have these people who come into the house . . . in . . . out . . . in . . . out. They don't live here, so I must watch them. My new Shepherd friends, Rayne, Crieff, Scotia, and Edin, all help me.

However, they don't bark much at these folks. They stop the minute they come in. Not me! I stick with the job! Then these people just laugh. Americans are different. However, I learned these people who come in and out are charged with taking care of us and working at dog school. They are very nice people and good friends.

They have toys galore here. Auntie Ann has even bought me some new toys. She said something about needing "tougher" toys for me. I guess the German Shepherds aren't as tough as I am. After all, I *am* Scottish, you know. One of Auntie Ann's students brought me a new tough toy as a welcome present. I like getting presents. I will share—well, *most* of the time—with my new best friends. I have lots of new friends, and I can outrun them all—well, *almost* all of them.

There is a Beagle/Pug mix named "Bernard" who thinks he is hot stuff. He can run fast, so I have to work on that one. We run, wrestle, tug, and play with the toys after we are finished with class. Bernard is little, so he can turn really tight corners and outrun most of us, but I am learning. He really is the fastest, so I guess he really *is* hot stuff. However, I'm working on it.

Auntie Marcia has two special friends, Scotia and Tay. There is another German Shepherd named "Rayne"; I mentioned her briefly before. She is so wise. Rayne knows everything and is kind enough to share it with me. She is fun to play with, too, but so are all the other German Shepherd Dogs here. Then there is Uncle Roger's and Auntie Ann's son, Auntie Marcia's brother, Clark, and his family. The mother in that family is Marilynn, and there are two short humans—Rayne told me they are called "kids" or "children"—Lauren and Amanda. Lauren is the older one, and Amanda is the shorter and younger one. They come to visit us sometimes.

I get to ride in the car to do errands. I get to ride shotgun. That means I ride in the front seat on the passenger side. Rayne, who knows everything, told me it comes from the Old West, when this country had stagecoaches pulled by horses. I didn't tell her that I didn't know what a "stagecoach" was. I do know what a "horse" is. I guess I'll find out what a stagecoach is at school. It's fun riding in the front seat. I keep the road clear of rabbits! I noticed there were no sheep here. Maybe I have just not found them yet, but, frankly, there is so much going on here, so much to explore, I am nay[10] caring.

I'm getting lots of jobs here. I have to exercise four German Shepherd Dogs by running their legs off. I have to watch the house. I alert the German Shepherds, and they go on guard. They like that because *I* make all the decisions about who just needs announcing that they are here and who needs more intense guarding duty. When these humans get sick, I have to watch over them, making sure they get their medicine and that they are protected when they are sleeping. I also keep the deer out of the yard . . . and the rabbits, squirrels, stray cats, and any other wildlife.

I have taken Uncle Roger off his feet, and I almost took Auntie Ann off her feet chasing a deer. I didn't want them to think I couldn't get the job done! They were both muttering that, in all the years, none of the German Shepherd Dogs had ever done that. I guess that proves that, although the German Shepherd Dogs are bigger than I am, Border Collies are quicker. Surprise! It's all about surprise!

I also have my therapy duties. I have to make sure everyone—dogs and humans—are in a good mood. Auntie Ann says I'm very funny, complex (I think that means "smart" *and* "good"), adorable,

---

10 See Miste's Vocabulary—Chapter 22

and destructive. She says I have destroyed more stuff in the past three months than the Shepherds have in the last ten years! And then she said I fit in here like a glove, and the Shepherds all love me, and all the people love me. Do you think that's why they say a Border Collie is not a dog for everyone? Well, I wouldn't *want* to be a "dog for everyone." Wouldn't that be boring!

CHAPTER 4

DID I TELL YOU?

Did I tell you Rayne had an accident? She had gone outside for a while, and one of the other dogs ran into her. It must have caught her just wrong because she came in unable to walk on one of her legs. Even though she couldn't walk on four legs, she controlled everything from where she was lying down. She is kind enough to let you know that, when you make a mistake, you will be in trouble with our humans.

I know that I'm learning to pay attention to her. Scotia thinks she walks on water. All the other German Shepherds think so, too. She is the boss of us, for sure. She has a way of making her point. She is loving and kind, but you sure get her point! She doesn't have cancer. She has been tested twice for that. She has gone to the vet a lot. She has had tons of tests. They just can't figure out what is wrong with that leg. She can get around on three legs. Of course, she isn't as fast as I am, so that is another job I have. I have to protect Rayne from getting run into by other dogs.

Uncle Roger had to go to Kosovo to accredit a journalism school. While he was gone, Clark, Marilynn, Lauren, and Amanda came for the day. It was a surprise. I had never played with short people—Rayne called them "kids." I'd met them, and I'd seen them, but I had not played with them. The taller one, Lauren, said she liked me a lot. She thought I was very pretty. I felt good. I chased balls for them and showed how fast I could run. I gave them kisses and told them how cute they were. Auntie Ann said I did a good job. I was glad to help.

We added another dog to the family. Well, he was already in the family, but he was new to me. Evidently, as Rayne told it, his story is this: Rayne knows everything here—only she is not as old as the Wise Old Goat. Rayne is like a historian. She collects all the news and stories from everyone, but she knew this story personally because Crieff was her litter brother. In case you're not a dog person, a brother is a dog with the same parents as you but is born at a different time . . . maybe even a year or two or more older or younger than you are. A litter brother not only has the same parents but is born at the same time you are, so you grew up from day one together. Rayne says Crieff was a wonderful brother. He was fun-loving, he loved people and other dogs, and he was very smart.

One day, Auntie Ann got a call from a minister she knew. The minister needed a special dog for a woman who needed a service dog. She wanted one of Auntie Ann's and Uncle Roger's puppies. She said that this woman really needed a good service dog and that this woman would be an excellent home for such a dog. Auntie Ann said she would meet with the woman.

They met. The interview went okay. Auntie Ann relied heavily on what the minister had told her, because this woman was from out of town . . . in fact, from clear across the country . . . and there was no way of checking up on her very deeply. Crieff went to live with this woman. Since they were clear across the country, news became sparse. However, a year later, this woman decided to move here, and she joined the training school. Auntie Ann was thrilled, but she wasn't prepared for what she saw. Crieff came in. He was depressed, fearful of everything, and defensive. This woman was way too harsh with him. She offered no praise for anything, even when Crieff did it right. She physically hit him often. On questioning, she was not feeding him high-quality food. Crieff was way too thin. She took him to places he was not prepared to go with the training he had received; his training had been inadequate. This resulted in Crieff panicking in stores and getting kicked out, which resulted in this woman taking her wrath out on poor Crieff.

Auntie Ann offered to buy Crieff back from this woman, but she wouldn't do it. Auntie Ann offered free extra lessons to help this woman, but she wouldn't do that, either. The situation dragged on for many months. One day, this woman called Auntie Ann. She was very angry. She said Crieff had snapped at a child who lived next door to her, and if Auntie Ann didn't come right now and get him out of her house, she was going to take him to the pound.

Auntie Ann went immediately. When Crieff saw her, he was ecstatic. Auntie Ann told the woman she would not leave until this woman signed over Crieff's papers to her. The woman said she would send them later. Auntie Ann insisted she would not leave until the woman found Crieff's papers and signed them over to Auntie Ann. To emphasize the point, Auntie Ann sat down in a nearby chair. Immediately, she had an 80-pound German Shepherd Dog named Crieff in her lap!

Crieff put his huge paws, one on either side of Auntie Ann's head, and started kissing her face. He scooched up against her as close as he could get. He was begging her to take him with her. He was begging her not to leave him here! Auntie Ann gave him a hug and peered around him to reinforce her position with this woman. The woman disappeared into the next room and appeared a couple of minutes later with the papers. She signed them over in front of Auntie Ann. Crieff was still hugging Auntie Ann as tightly as he could. Now Auntie Ann had to get up . . . a rather difficult task with a full-grown German Shepherd Dog refusing to let go. Auntie Ann entered into a private conversation with Crieff, explaining the problem. She asked how could they leave and go home if Auntie Ann couldn't get up? She explained that he was, after all, a King's Pride German Shepherd Dog and needed to be brave and strong. He should know she was not going to leave him, but she needed him to walk to the car on his four feet because she could not carry him!

Something got through to Crieff, and, reluctantly, he slid to the floor, now hugging Auntie Ann's leg. That was a start. Auntie Ann scooped up the papers and half walked, dragging her one leg, to which Crieff was attached, to the door. As they cleared the door, Crieff let go of Auntie Ann's leg and sprang to the lead, pulling her down the walk to the car. When the door of the car was opened, he leapt in and scrambled away from the door as far into the car as he could go. They left and came home.

Crieff was free, but he was so traumatized that he could not do anything but tremble and huddle into the ground, wherever he was. Auntie Ann decided he needed to know he was back home.

He needed to remember his puppyhood. He needed to understand that this past year had been very bad—but that now that chapter in his life was over. He was home, and he was safe. Auntie Ann put him next to his family—his mother, brother, and sister. He wasn't asked to do anything from training or school. He ate good food. He gained weight. He played, and after a year, he was smiling and his old happy self once again . . . but it took a year to do that. Then, and only then, was he ready to start schooling again. At first, very slowly, and only when he showed eagerness to go on, was the next step started. You could see the difference in his face in the photos.

I knew him after his recovery. I loved playing with him. Rayne said he didn't like to talk about when he'd been gone from here because it gave him nightmares, so we never talked about it. He was funny and loved to play. He made me realize how lucky I was to have come here. I could have wound up with a mean owner like that, or an owner who just tied me out in the backyard on a chain all day, or put me in a crate all day, or didn't feed me. I missed Grace, but I didn't have time to dwell on it. I could not change Grace's dying, so I was lucky I had wound up here, just like Crieff was lucky to be home again.

CHAPTER 5

MY SCHOOL

I was still in full school. I just never knew how much there was to learn. I had to learn how to pass a Canine Good Citizenship Test, and then I had to pass a Therapy Dogs International Test, and then I would be an official therapy dog. Then, I would be able to go into schools, nursing homes, hospitals, courtrooms, and every other place to help people in lots of ways. First, I had to pass the test. Each test is on different subjects, and, if you didn't get them right, then you flunked.

If I got tired of sitting and wanted to move along or do something else, OH-HA! I was supposed to just stay there in that spot. Boring, just plain boring. Then, I was supposed to sit when they stopped walking, even when you were on a good trail or a friend was up ahead of you. Auntie Ann started saying, "Control your energy." Well, I was controlling my energy. I was using it to visit my friends! I had to learn to walk, sit, down, and stand on wire grating; on some slippery plastic tarps that moved when you walked on them; on a narrow board high up off the ground; walk up to umbrellas that would jump out at you and go "Boo!" Then there was the sway bridge, the swing plank, and the dark, l-o-n-g tunnels. It was hard. Very hard. Very, very hard. We had to learn to sit and stay while a bunch of people swamped you, all getting their hands on you at once. They dropped loud things behind you, made you walk through yummy treats on the floor without getting any, and drop instantly to the ground when they said "down." I heard there were even harder things in the more-advanced classes. I didn't even want to think about those.

I had to learn to walk no more than six inches away from my human's left knee, and when my human stopped walking, I had to sit immediately. That meant that, first, I had to learn how much "six inches" was. Then, there are all these sounds humans use. How many of you know a foreign language? I have to sit, or down, or stand, not moving any feet, no matter what else is moving or happening around us. You must come when you are called. That's hard. I have to hold still while they cut my toenails! I don't like to have my toenails clipped! Auntie Ann says, "Forget it. You have to do this." You have to get your teeth, your eyes, and your ears all cleaned and examined. I mean, it is really hard work—*exhausting* work—and some of it is no fun at all!

Some of it is fun. Well, I have to be honest—*a lot* of it is really fun. Like when we are learning to tunnel under everyone's legs. Everyone is standing in a circle with their legs apart, with their dogs sitting by their left side. Then we dogs go through human legs around the circle or in a straight line, lickety-split. You can't stop to say "Hi" to any of the dogs in the circle, either. You have to go through the legs and around back to your human's side. Oh, yes, and you can't *ever* bark in class, or when you're working, or when you're in your crate. See what I mean?

I had to learn to bow, give a high-five, and do a figure eight around my human's legs. I'm learning to climb into a chair when told—but not *unless* I am told to do it; get off the chair immediately when told; accept full-body hugs from anyone big or little and sit still while they do it. In agility, I am learning how to go over, through, and around the dog-walk, tunnels, A-frame, chute, teeter-totter, tire jump, platform jump, swing plank, crawl tunnel, hoop tunnel, and all sorts of things. I love agility. People say I took to it like a duck to water. I haven't seen any ducks in my agility class. I guess they're in an upper level.

Then I am learning how to pull a wagon. It's called "carting." The carts and wagons are all decorated. A lot of this learning is part of what they call Drill Team. My friends are members. It's made up of families who enjoy working with their dogs. The team members meet at the school for practice; many of them come several times a week. They work on dog-obedience skills and musical numbers that are almost like dancing with your human.

The team presents a major show in December at the school, and it also goes to other places to perform: schools, nursing homes, parks, parades, and so forth.

I began my drill-team career one Saturday afternoon. We usually had our morning and afternoon classes on Saturday. We do six hours of classes on Saturday. Then we go home, and, usually, that is all of our outside work for Saturday. But not that Saturday. We got in the car again and left. We arrived at this building; I started seeing all my friends going in, and then we went in. It was like a big hotel where senior citizens live.

There were my friends. It was sort of like a surprise party to me, but, then, every one of us was on command, and we had to behave, because everyone was watching every move we made. Then our drill music started, and we started to do the drills. Jordan, a friend and team member, worked me; so did Auntie Ann and Auntie Marcia. I had to sit out only one drill, but I wanted to do that one as well, so I put my foot through the ring gate and tried to catch everyone as they passed by. Auntie Ann and Auntie Marcia thought that was funny. Some of the audience thought I was funny, too. Everyone said what a good job I had done. Everyone wanted to pet me. I had to be on my best behavior, and I was. It was *so* much fun. I was so tired, though, that on the last drill, when I was supposed to sit, I lay down. I *never* lie down when I am out.

I don't know why they were all laughing about the Border Collie they wore out. Crieff was there. He wasn't as tired as I was because he had taken a nap earlier in the day. I don't take naps. I might miss something.

Then, there are what humans call "the house manners." You can't surf the counters and tables. Well, that's where the humans put the food. What are you supposed to do when you are hungry? Let me tell you what I used to do, even though it was wrong.

It was, after all, the holidays. Are you not supposed to get treats—lots of treats—during the holidays? Everyone else was enjoying good things to eat. Yes, they shared the turkey, and well, they just forgot that piece. It was a bone, after all. It was a perfectly good bone, and they were throwing it away?! What kind of waste is that in a world where hunger still exists? I was being frugal—waste not, want not. I must admit the trip to the vet was not fun. I did not like it one bit. And now, even though we have just gone through all the *Be of good cheer, and love and kindness, and good will to all, forgiveness, and all that*—well, let me tell you, talk is cheap! They are watching me like a Bald Eagle after a poor fish and come sweeping in to bang the trash can or the counter and say harsh words to me like "Leave it!" or "Out of that!" So, I ask you: Where are the good cheer, the treats, and the feeling that good things are there when you're smart enough to figure out how to get them and that they are yours for the taking?

Here is how Auntie Ann described this situation:

"Somehow, Miste got the pantry door opened and got into the trash, where a turkey leg had been put into a plastic bag—then in another plastic bag—and into the trash. Little Miss eats anything and is always—hungry roly-poly . . . ate it. . . . Well, anyway, we *think* that because we have not been able to find the turkey-leg bone anywhere. So, after a night of feeding her bread and milk and staying up to watch her, we took her in . . . that very, very snowy, slick morning . . . with no vet at Keene Street, and only one could make it in that New Year's Day at Buttonwood. She was X-rayed; there was debris of some sort in her, but they could not say what, and we were advised to take her home and watch her. So far, she is okay, still pooping, not throwing up, and acting normally. I think she will be fine and am hoping her digestive juices have broken down the bone. It *was* cooked, and our girl has undergone some strict stealing lessons, which she has not enjoyed. It involved some harsh—very harsh—words, which Miste is not used to hearing."

Well, what do they expect? I was hungry, and nobody was there to tell me not to do it. There was no supervision or instruction. So, once again, the humans were wrong. But they are the boss.

Let's get back to other house manners. You have to sit and wait in the car, even though the door is open, until you are invited out. You must not chase the deer, squirrels, rabbits, or wild cats.

You can chase the German Shepherds. You must sit when you approach a door and wait to be invited through, and then you must sit on the other side until told to walk on or are given some other instruction. You must not pull on the leash when walking. You can chase the GSDs. Humans go on and on with what you can and cannot do. On the other hand, I have observed canines in class who have not learned or have not been taught these manners, and their lives are miserable. Many of them lose their homes and, in some cases, their lives.

While I really thought the humans were wrong, at *this* time of year, they could have been more understanding. For example, they could have offered other treats and included me in more family activities or provided other activities that would have been fun, with alternative treats that would not have led to an awful visit to the vet, but I get some of it. While delicious, turkey, chicken, and other meat bones are dangerous for us canines. Bone shards can tear your intestines apart, and you could bleed to death. I also understand now that my humans were panic-stricken about my health and safety. So, like most things, it's complicated. I think the best path is just to try to follow your human's rules, whether you think they are right or wrong, and remember, they are the boss. Remember, the boss is still the boss. Enough of that. Of course, you *do* know I am the personal German Shepherd Dog exercise trainer.

I can take on four at a time. I can wear them out in our very large, fenced field in no time and be ready for more. I will get them in shape in no time. In other words, I have school, but I also have a job. I can handle it. After all, I am a Border Collie.

CHAPTER 6

SNOW ADVENTURES

It is snowing outside and cold. We have all had to come in. We are glad we are in because it is miserable to be so cold, but it also means it's boring to be in because we can't run and tear around, chasing each other and playing. Sooooo, sometimes we can get Rayne to tell us stories. Rayne is kind of a historian here. She has the best stories. They are about dogs who have lived in this family, giving us a history. So, today Rayne agreed to tell us a story. We all settled in to listen.

Rayne began: "I remember hearing stories about a really bad snowstorm when our human mom was a 12-year-old kid. Her family lived in Traverse City, Michigan, on a 17-mile peninsula jutting out into Grand Traverse Bay. Their backyard sloped down into the bay. In front of the house was a large front yard, bordering on the peninsula road that ran around the edge of the peninsula. Across the road, open fields stretched into deep woods. The peninsula was sparsely inhabited by people but had bears, bobcats, wolverines, foxes, deer, opossums, raccoons, and the usual rabbits, squirrels, and who knows what else. No one had fenced-in yards. Dogs ran loose. They mostly got along. Occasional tiffs were very rarely serious. Dogs never ran off or got lost. What do you think?! These are country dogs with good noses, and they know how to use them. These are dogs who lived loose all the time. They knew how to handle it . . . most of the time.

"The family consisted of our human mom (Ann), age 12, her mom, Blanch, and her dad, Will, an 18-month-old German Shepherd Dog named 'Ricky,' and a black cat with yellow eyes named 'Punky.'

"It was 8 o'clock in the evening . . . a time when Ricky and Punky were let outside to potty for the last time before bedtime. There was a large snowstorm due to begin that night, and the snow was already beginning to fall. They were expecting eight to twelve inches of accumulation. There was already about four inches of snow on the ground from a previous snowfall.

"The new snow was exciting to the young and curious Ricky, who burst through the door and out into the snow, snapping and jumping into the new, falling snow, catching the flakes before they hit the ground.

"Punky, on the other hand, was disgusted. She was an unusual cat in that she would wade out into the bay water, hunting fish, or chase soap bubbles and water down the drain in the basement laundry room. She looked at snow with disdain, shaking her paws if any snow got onto them, and that is what she did this evening. She took her time standing in the doorway, devising her strategy to get to her potty area and back with the least amount of exposure. When she had assured herself that the porch was protected, she slowly walked out on it and crouched down as cats do to plan her next move, determined to keep as much snow off her plush black coat as possible.

"Meanwhile, Ricky was bounding around the yard, rooting in the snow, rolling in it, and, in general, trying very hard to get as much snow on his coat as possible. Suddenly, Ricky's nose went into the snow. He snorted with mock seriousness as he began to follow the underlying tracks through the snow, out of the yard, and beyond. *Good riddance*, thought Punky. She sure didn't need him jumping around her, splashing snow all over her.

"Inside, the family continued getting ready for the storm. They collected water in the bathtubs, sinks, and washing machine in case the water lines froze or broke. They stacked wood by the fireplace to have it ready in case the furnace went out or the power failed. They got out flashlights and candles and prepared clothing, so that they could dress in warmer and warmer layers, boots, extra blankets, and items for food preparation—in case the power went out, the pipes burst, or both.

"Five minutes after being let out, Punky was in the window above the kitchen sink, where our mom (Ann) was helping with the dishes and food preparation. Punky was demanding to come back in. When the door was opened, she rushed inside, vocalizing her displeasure with the storm, the snow, and the cold. She immediately went to the stuffed chair by the fireplace and proceeded to clean herself all over to get every trace of snow off herself.

"Ricky was nowhere in sight. Not a surprise. Actually, it was good. The family was not ready for bed yet, and he could wear himself out and then sleep better tonight, so no one would have to get up and wait for him to go in the middle of the night. Then an hour passed with no familiar scratch at the door from Ricky. The storm had picked up considerably in strength.

"The wind whipped the ground snow and drove the now-very-heavy downpour of new snow into a visibility of only two or three feet. It would get worse. Will, Mom's dad, let out his shrill, very loud whistle for Ricky. No bouncy cream-and-black sable German Shepherd Dog leapt into sight. Except for the wind, the world was silent. Will tried again in fifteen minutes. Still Nothing. Another fifteen minutes went by, and still nothing. Concern and worry took over, and Will prepared to go out. He laid out a large flashlight, checking the batteries and replacing them (he was not quite sure how old they were), rope, and an axe, all of which he attached to a toolbelt. After a cup of hot coffee, he started out, following the now-very-faint trail across the road and into the woods.

"Knowing the snow was building quickly, Will marked the trees with his axe so he could find his way back. As he followed the tracks, he was aware they were fading as the wind whipped up the new and blowing snow. He called for Ricky every few steps, but it was like the wind shoved his voice right back down his throat. It was slow going in the strong wind and blowing snow, and the trail was fading, always fading. Then, as he was about to give up and turn back, he thought he heard a sound. He realized his voice wasn't working, so he made and issued his very special, very shrill whistle. This time it was answered with Ricky's very distinctive bark and a crying, painful sound Will had never heard before. They answered each other until Will found Ricky.

"Ricky's left front foot was caught in a large, very rusty old bear trap chained to the thick branch of an old fallen tree. Try as he might, Will yanked at the chain but could not yank or cut the chain free. He would have to cut it off with the small axe. That took a lot of energy, and after a long time, he was now sweating and worried about getting wet and cold from the inside out. The snow had thickened even more, and the wind had created blizzard conditions. Baby-bite by baby-bite, Will chopped through the branch, and he was able to get the chain loose from the tree. Now he was faced with how to get Ricky home.

"Ricky could not walk with that rusty bear trap on his foot. Will had only one choice. He had to carry him. It took him almost half an hour to get Ricky on his shoulders, around his neck, and standing again. The good side was that Ricky was young, still slender in build, and not as heavy as he would be when he was older. At last, Will struggled to his feet with the help of a small tree, Ricky screaming in pain every time the trap shifted on his foot. The wound bled and dripped onto all of Will's clothes, hands, arms, boots, and even into his hair and hat.

"Will had marked the trees fairly close together, and for a while, he could follow them because the tree branches made a sort of umbrella, broke some of the wind, and sheltered the ground against the snow. As the storm progressed, however, the marked trees became increasingly difficult to find. The snow had filled his boot prints, and the wind had erased all trace of them. The wind had also driven snow into the crevices of the axe marks on the trees, making them impossible to find. Now he had to rely on his sense of direction. He reached an open space. He knew it was an open space because of the increased force of the wind as it hit him, and the snow stung his face. He tied his rope to the tree next to him and went out into what seemed like nowhere. Then he tried to go to the right and found more trees . . . back to the original tree and go to the left . . . more trees. He tried once more to see how large this clearing was and went forward until he found a tree. This was the road!

"There was only one road on the peninsula, so now he had to guess which way. He mulled it over as he untied the rope from the original tree. Half guessing and half following his gut feeling, he started out. He walked from one side of the road to the other in zigzag fashion down the road from one tree line to the other. That pattern helped him keep from walking in circles and working his way down the road. He couldn't stop. He felt that, if he did stop, it wouldn't be long before the storm overwhelmed him. After what seemed like an eternity, he thought he saw a light hinting dimly through the snow. He didn't want to get lost, though, so he zigzagged on for about twenty more yards until he was certain it was a light . . . a real light . . . and then he headed straight for it.

"When he stumbled through the back door and fell to the floor, Ricky screamed in pain, which brought our mom and her mom, Blanch, running into an awful sight. They dragged Will's feet in to get the door shut, leaving the wind and snow outside. Then they started pulling and lifting the wet, heavy dog off Will's shoulders, Ricky screaming all the while.

"Then they started pulling and ripping the wet, cold clothes off Will and pulling on the dry ones that had been warming by the fireplace, all the while discussing how to get the trap off Ricky's foot and cleaning Ricky's wounds. Next was getting some hot coffee into Will's stomach. While Will was sipping the coffee, their attention turned to Ricky, lying on the floor, not moving. While they were discussing how to get the trap off, Blanch and our mom (Ann) started working on cleaning the wounded paw by pouring hydrogen peroxide on the foot and soaking it. Then they started prying off the trap jaws. It took them more than an hour to get the trap off, but after working on the rust, oiling the joints, cleaning off whatever rust they could, and prying with all their might, they finally managed to get it open enough to get Ricky's paw out. A call to the vet gave them an outline of a plan until they could get through the storm and get Ricky to the vet.

"The storm would last the rest of the night and until noon the next day. Because of that—and despite the fact that the chains had been on the tires of the car for more than a month already—the vet visit had to wait for the snowplow to come through. That didn't happen until after dark . . . too late to make it to town.

"Finally, the next day, they were able to load Ricky into the car and get him to the veterinarian. The vet started Ricky on antibiotics and laid out a routine for tending his wounds. He lost part of one toe. Even with that, everyone felt Ricky was lucky that his wounds were not graver.

"Punky ignored Ricky even more than usual. It was clear she considered him way too unintelligent for her to associate herself with him about anything. You would never, *ever* catch her out in that storm, let alone that far out in the woods—and caught in a bear trap! As far as she was concerned, he deserved everything he got . . . the poor fool."

What fun it was to listen to Rayne's stories on a day when we had to mostly stay inside. I loved Rayne's stories. They let me in on the family history. Rayne is sort of like the Wise Old Goat was in Scotland.

CHAPTER 7

ORPHAN PUPPIES

It's me . . . Miste. I don't doubt anymore that I am needed here. I am the official cheerer-upper.

We have had a tragedy. Tay, the mother of the new puppies we have, died. She had cancer, which no one knew about, and evidently, the hormones from having the puppies worked like pouring gasoline on a fire. So, we have been raising orphan puppies.

They now have proper names. "King's Pride" is our dog-family name. So, their names are King's Pride's Tay's Garrioch. We are calling her "Gerrie" for short and King's Pride's Tay's Mindin. Auntie Marcia found that *mindin* is Scottish for a "gift given as a remembrance of the giver." A gift from Tay is a reminder of Tay. Garrioch is the chapel Alec helped find a few years ago. It is where Auntie Ann's grandfather's birth is recorded.

So, everyone is very busy making formula and taking care of the wee ones. They are eating formula with Knox gelatin, evaporated milk, water, egg yolk slightly cooked but liquid, baby vitamins, and Karo syrup, Gerber's baby meat strained, and Gerber's baby cereal rice. I understand from Rayne that the puppies hold their urine until either their mom licks their bare tummies or the humans use a wet washcloth to wipe the puppies' bare tummies to get them to urinate and poop. That way, their nest stays dry and clean.

I haven't been able to see them yet, but Rayne, the one who knows *everything*, says my turn will come.

Auntie Ann has been pretty sick. Larry, her doctor, is trying to keep her out of the hospital. She has acute bronchitis. She has to stay sitting all day and night, even when she sleeps.

I am still in school. There is a lot to learn, and I really love it. Auntie Ann says I try very hard, and I am learning very well. I just never knew how much there was to learn! I like agility best. I am learning how to pass a Canine Good Citizenship Test, and then I have to pass a therapy-dog test. Then I will be an official therapy dog.

We got hopeful news about Rayne, the one who knows everything. She had to have a second operation for more biopsies. However, they showed no signs of cancer, either. She is on antibiotics and pain medication. I don't know what the next step is. She sure has something wrong with that leg. She hasn't been able to walk on it since October. She gets around quite well on three legs, however. She is really smart.

Now officially I took over Rayne's job; I keep the deer out of our yard! I also keep the rabbits, squirrels, and stray cats out of the yard . . . just in case you forgot.

Crieff and I are going out to play outside. Yesterday, I had a wonderful time. I splashed in a mud puddle until I was brown instead of black and white! It was so much fun! Then Charlie gave me a bath. Yuck! Crieff didn't get even a speck of mud on himself. Oh, well—he missed all the fun!!! Maybe the puddle will be out there again today.

CHAPTER 8

SEASONS

The snowstorms have started coming! It's still February, and my, oh, my—what a lot of snow we had. It closed down the major highway for the first time in history. Of course, you must realize that the history here is not nearly as old as the history in Scotland, but it was certainly longer than either my lifetime or those of any of the humans we know.

Here, I was up to my belly in snow! It was really fun to run around in. We went out into a blizzard, with the wind howling and blowing snow, which made you feel all rugged. It made me think of Ricky's snowstorm, even if we were only in the backyard. Scotia, Crieff, Mindin, Gerrie, and Edin got to run around in this stuff, too. We had a ball. However, Auntie Ann, Auntie Marcia, and Uncle Roger couldn't get to town or even out of our driveway for days because the snow was so deep. They had to bring two trucks—one to plow out the driveway and the other to pull the first truck out of the drifts.

I was afraid we would run out of dog cookies, but we didn't. I was told we had planned for the storm ahead of time. Of course, we had to cancel classes. For a while there, I couldn't keep up with what we were supposed to be learning.

The snow was beautiful for all that trouble; it was all white and fluffy. When you looked down the drive or in the trees, it was all blue, gray, and white . . . all soft, smudgy and very lovely. Auntie Marcia couldn't get to school, so she had to work very hard at home, but I kept her spirits up by bringing her toys and insisting she take play breaks. A Border Collie's work is never done.

With all the cold and snowy weather, we got to hear more of Rayne's stories. Rayne tells us lots of stories about the dogs in our canine family. I've already told you some of them. This one started when Auntie Ann was a kid. Her dad, Will, loved horses and dogs. I've told you about Ricky, their German Shepherd, in the snowstorm. Well, then there was the time Ricky was stolen. The family was living in Michigan, on that seventeen-mile peninsula where Ricky had gotten caught in a bear trap in a snowstorm.

Ricky loved everything. He loved all people, dogs, cats . . . just all of everything! His trust was absolute. He trusted everyone about everything. It happened so quickly.

It was the middle of the day. A delivery man, new on the job, saw it all. He was not familiar with the neighborhood and did not know who was who, which dogs belonged where and with whom, or what their personalities were, but he did know that all the dogs were allowed to run loose. Ricky had to go potty, and, so, the family let him out into the yard. The yard was half an acre in size and sat back off the road about fifty yards. The delivery man had pulled to the side of the road to check out addresses and where they were. He saw the car drive up and stop. He saw the back door of the car open, and the dog ran over to greet these new people. He saw the German Shepherd Dog climb into the car. The car door closed, and the car drove off. The delivery man just thought the dog was getting into his own car, but, of course, that was not the case.

Immediately, notices were put in newspapers. This event was years ago, and there were not very many German Shepherd Dogs in the area. The first report they had about Ricky was 20 miles away, around the bay, north of Acme. Ricky must have escaped from his captors. Ricky's family drove around the woods in that area, with Auntie Ann calling and Will whistling for him, to no avail. They went home after leaving posters with Ricky's picture and contact information on them.

A few days later, another report was phoned in from a spot about five miles closer to home. Again, Ricky's family went out to hunt for him. Again, nothing. Sadly, Ricky's family again went home without Ricky.

Then, a few days later, another report was phoned in from a man who said he had seen Ricky. He said that, at first, he thought it was a wolf, but as he steadied up his rifle to aim, he saw a flash around the dog's neck and remembered the ad Ricky's family had put in the paper. He realized the animal was not a wolf, but a German Shepherd Dog. He said he lowered the rifle and called to the dog. The dog listened, hesitating at the sound of his name. He decided not to trust this man who used his name; he turned and ran off. Ricky's family again hunted; Auntie Ann called until she was hoarse and desperate. Will whistled, but all was to no avail.

It was suppertime; the family saw a roadside restaurant and decided to get dinner there. As they ordered and ate dinner, they struck up a conversation with the waitress and told her how gentle Ricky was, even if he did look like a wolf. They told her how he loved children and how he was probably very hungry, might be thirsty, and was definitely very scared. They told her how sad they were because they had been so unsuccessful. But the waitress saw a glimmer of hope—Ricky appeared to be working himself closer and closer to home. If anyone was still wondering if a dog could really do this—find his way home from a place he had never been before—Ricky was proving he possibly could. They were also encouraged by the fact that the reports had had correct information in them—that this dog was, indeed, Ricky. Ricky was alive and moving toward home.

It was a couple of days later that the waitress from the restaurant called. "I have Ricky in my backyard. My children are feeding him and giving him water. He wouldn't let me near him, but he accepted the children, just like you said he would."

Will got into the car and rolled down the windows, as the car had no air conditioning. Will drove to the waitress's house and turned into her driveway, which ran beside her house to the garage, which was detached and to the left rear of the house about 20 feet. Ricky was at the back of the yard, eating out of the hands of a boy about nine and a girl about twelve. He had not paid any attention to Will's arrival because his attention was totally focused on the food and the children.

Will said quietly, "Well, Ricky." The dog instantly recognized Will's voice and whirled around with his whole body. Without hesitation—even for a moment—Ricky burst into a dead run, past Will and straight for the car. How did he know the car was there?

He sailed into the air aiming to go through the open window. How did he know the windows were down and open? Everyone gasped, frozen in their spot.

Once in the car, Ricky whirled back around and sat in the front seat, not about to move and with the biggest grin on his face, which was filled with complete joy. Will thanked the waitress profusely and insisted she accept a bit of reward. Then he brought Ricky home for a jubilant reunion.

Another story Rayne told was about King.

Every morning, King and Auntie Ann took a walk around the lake in a park at the end of the street where Auntie Ann and Uncle Roger lived at the Air Force base. The lake was about twelve acres in size, with the park around it. The whole thing was about forty to fifty acres. It served as the dump area for bombs, if they ever needed it; so far, they had not. So, it served as a park for Air Force families. King loved his walk every morning.

A new family had moved into the downstairs apartments. They had a large family with a girl, named Kay, starting kindergarten, a boy, Johnny, who was a year younger than Kay, and a teenage girl who had disabilities. The family had fallen in love with King. They offered to buy him. Of course, it was explained that King was part of the family, and, as far as Auntie Ann and Uncle Roger were concerned, it would be like selling your only child.

It was the end of August, and school had just started. Johnny just could not understand why he couldn't go to school with Kay. He was very jealous of her, and, at just a year younger, he was very competitive. Their mother, Georgianna, begged Auntie Ann to let Johnny go on the two-hour morning walk with King, so Johnny could have something special to do, since he couldn't go to school with Kay. Auntie Ann felt sorry for the little boy, so she agreed to do it. For several months, they walked, no matter the weather. Johnny was a mischievous young man and often difficult to keep track of, but for two hours every morning, King and Auntie Ann did it.

One afternoon, Auntie Ann was asked to bring King and go to the park for a moving-away picnic for a mutual friend and her two children, who were about the same ages as Johnny and Kay. This was a familiar and frequent activity for those whose spouses were in the Air Force. A standard answer to anyone who asked you to do something—serve on a committee or organize something—was just one word . . . "Figmo." It was Air Force talk: *"Forget It. I've Got My Orders!"* But this was a party.

So, that made three women, four children, and a German Shepherd Dog, who was having a ball playing with the children. They had eaten the picnic fare, and the dog and children were running and playing, while the women were sitting at the picnic table, watching the kids, sipping their coffee, and chatting. Johnny was jumping over a branch that had fallen from a tree. He tripped and fell; a piece of broken branch punctured his leg. The women doctored it a bit, got the bleeding stopped, packed up the picnic items, and left for home.

It was about 10 a.m. the next day when there was a knock on the front door of the apartment. Not expecting anybody, Auntie Ann put King in his crate, so that his wolf-like appearance wouldn't scare anyone. She hushed him and basically told him she would handle it. Then she answered the door. There stood two uniformed Air Force police officers holding heavy chains and very heavy ropes.

"May I help you?" Auntie Ann asked.

"We've come to take your dog in," one of the officers said gruffly.

"Why?" Auntie Ann asked.

"Because he bit a boy yesterday," the officer said.

"My dog did not bite anyone," Auntie Ann said, staring the officer right in the eyes.

"I'm sorry, Ma'am, but we have our orders," the officer replied.

"My dog is a show dog, and what you plan on doing to him—with your ropes and chains—will ruin his show temperament and his feelings about strangers. You will take this dog out of here (now through gritted teeth) *over my dead body . . .* "

The officers were visibly taken aback. Auntie Ann was eight months pregnant. Everyone just stood there a minute while the situation sank in. "I want to call my husband," announced Auntie Ann. "You wait here!"

She closed the door and locked it, leaving them standing outside. She was not taking any chances. She called Uncle Roger. He said he would look into it and asked her to just wait for his call.

Auntie Ann returned to the door. "Come in, and sit down. My husband is looking into this and will call back in a few minutes. Meanwhile, we will wait."

They waited. While they waited, Auntie Ann found out some of the details of the accusation. It seemed that, after Johnny fell in the park yesterday, his mother, Georgianna, said he needed to go to the hospital, where it was decided that he needed a tetanus shot. However, it was after hours, and she could not get one until the next day—unless the puncture wound had been caused by an animal. So, Georgianna said King had bitten Johnny.

Auntie Ann assured the Air Force Police that King had not bitten anyone and that she knew a witness who could testify to that and exactly how the accident occurred. The phone rang. It was Air Force Police headquarters, wanting to speak to the officers. There was a short conversation, and the officers excused themselves and left.

Auntie Ann went directly downstairs, but Georgianna and Johnny were not at home. Auntie Ann waited and watched for two more hours. Meanwhile, Uncle Roger had called. He had essentially the same story Auntie Ann had been told and said that the police were going to investigate. Then a detective called Auntie Ann and asked for her side of the story.

Georgianna and Johnny came home, and Auntie Ann went immediately to see them. She explained what had happened. Georgianna emphatically said, "I certainly did not say that King bit Johnny! Why, I would *never* do that. I love that dog," she kept insisting.

Auntie Ann left. The next day was quiet, but the following morning, Auntie Ann looked out the window in time to see Georgianna and Johnny hurrying out the back door to the building. Auntie Ann quickly went to her front window, and, sure enough, there were the same two officers who had come before, getting heavy ropes and chains out of their van. She quickly locked the front door and called the detective she had spoken to two days ago.

Then came the knock at the door. "Just a minute," Auntie Ann called out. The detective on the phone overheard all this and interjected, "Let me speak to the officers, and then let's you and I talk about this after they leave."

Auntie Ann put King in the crate, opened the door, invited the officers in, and escorted them to the telephone. They left. Auntie Ann returned to the conversation with the detective. He said Georgianna was not backing off from her assertion that King had bitten Johnny. They had not been able to get in touch with the third-party witness yet. Auntie Ann told him Georgianna had assured her that she would never accuse King of biting Johnny. The detective told Auntie Ann he would continue to investigate.

The following day, the detective called again. He told Auntie Ann that he had gotten in contact with the third-party witness and that she had told exactly the same story that Auntie Ann had told. He wanted Auntie Ann to go downstairs and be in the apartment within earshot of Georgianna when she talked on the phone, and he would call her and try to make her say in front of Auntie Ann and the detective that King bit Johnny, if that was her story.

Auntie Ann knew Georgianna loved Auntie Ann's Scottish shortbread, so she went downstairs to ask if she could borrow enough sugar to make some shortbread she could share with Georgianna, who loved it so much that she would hide it from the rest of the family, so that she could have it all. So downstairs Auntie Ann went, sugar tin in hand.

When she heard the word "shortbread," Georgianna immediately welcomed Auntie Ann in and went to the cupboard for the sugar. The phone rang. Georgianna answered. Quickly, she realized who was calling. "I can't speak right now," she said.

The caller obviously kept insisting. This time, she said in an even more commanding tone, "I said that I can *not* speak with you right now. I will call you back." She hung up.

She reached for the sugar in the cupboard, and the phone rang again. She turned to Auntie Ann, saying, "You go on up, and I'll bring the sugar right away." The phone was still ringing.

"Oh, that's okay," Auntie Ann said, "I'll just sit here a minute. I'm a little out of breath."

The phone was ringing again, and Georgianna answered it. "Hello." Obviously, someone on the other end of the line was talking. Georgianna said, in a very pointed voice, "I told you— I'm busy and I cannot talk to you right now. Call me tomorrow." Then she hung up.

The next day, the detective called. He said it was obvious that Georgianna was lying about King's biting Johnny. The problem now was her husband's future. If Georgianna was found guilty of lying to the hospital, he would not get his upcoming promotion, and it probably would end his future as a career officer.

The detective asked if Auntie Ann and Uncle Roger would consider just letting her accusations stand . . . that it would not mean incarceration or any other punishment for King. But, Auntie Ann knew it would punish both King and his family, because it would end his show career, because a dog convicted of biting would be prohibited from showing. Auntie Ann said it would not be fair because King was totally innocent. There was a witness. King was nowhere near Johnny when he fell. They hung up.

A couple of hours later, the detective called again. This time, he wondered if Auntie Ann and Uncle Roger would consider this: The hospital regulations said "animal-inflicted wound." The detective said, "What if it were reported that King and Johnny were running and playing, and that King had accidentally stepped on Johnny's leg, causing Johnny to fall, and that's when the puncture wound happened. That would save the military career, King's career, and his reputation. It would probably be the best solution for the most people."

Auntie Ann and Uncle Roger thought about this. Although this was still a lie, it would affect five people's lives very deeply. Four of those people were innocent victims, just as King, Auntie Ann, and Uncle Roger were. King would be safe. King's life would not be changed. Uncle Roger and Auntie Ann agreed to do it.

Things were not quite the same after that. Johnny was not invited on King's walks anymore. Aside from an occasional "Hello" when unexpectedly passing in the front hall, the families did not speak.

Probably the most punishing for Georgianna was that Auntie Ann would not make shortbread for her anymore.

Rayne told another story about King, again from when he'd been at the Air Force base. Auntie Ann and Uncle Roger had an apartment on the second floor of the building. There were four apartments in each building, two upstairs and two downstairs. Each apartment had two bedrooms, one bathroom, a living/dining area and a kitchen/laundry. Sometimes a large family got two apartments on the ground floor; in circumstances such as these, there were three families in the building, instead of four. Such was the case at the time of this story.

The family living on the first floor had a sixteen-year-old boy who was enthralled with himself. He often made smart-alec remarks; he often made sarcastic and belittling comments about dogs in general and King in particular. His name was DJ. On this day, DJ and seven of his teenage friends were lounging on the front porch when Auntie Ann and King returned from their morning walk around the lake. In order to get into the building and up the stairs to the apartment, Auntie Ann had to go through these boys to get to the front door and into the main front hall. As they walked up to the porch, one young man said, "Hey, that's one handsome dog!" DJ said, "He's nothing. He's really stupid. He's a robot . . . punch the right buttons, and he does whatever you tell him to do."

Another of the teens said, "Oh, yeah? I wanna see that. Let's see ya do it." The sarcastic teen came over to King, who was standing quietly by Auntie Ann's side. "Down!" he bellowed at the Shepherd.

King looked up at him and then at Auntie Ann. His tongue rolled out of his mouth, and his face spread into a broad smile. His eyes twinkled. He just stood there, totally ignoring the bellowing teen.

"Down, down, down!" bellowed the teen, bending over the dog and gesturing to the ground.

King's eyes twinkled; he wagged his tail and lifted a paw in invitation to play.

The boys laughed. DJ scoffed, "Aw, he's just plain stupid."

Auntie Ann raised her eyebrows and very softly said, "Down."

The dog dropped instantly to the ground and stayed there until Auntie Ann whispered "stand."

King popped instantly to his feet and stood stock still. Auntie Ann whispered "front," and King whirled around to sit perfectly in front of Auntie Ann. Auntie Ann silently shifted her eyes to her right, and King immediately flashed around her right side and into a perfect straight sit at her left side, his eyes riveted on her, eagerly awaiting more directions.

"Wow" and other sounds of admiration and approval came from every teen on that porch—except DJ, who only snorted disdain. The boys all wanted to meet King and pet him. So, the next several minutes were spent in these introductions while DJ sulked at the end of the porch. The boys parted as King and Auntie Ann went inside and up the stairs.

In March, the season changed to early spring. April 3rd is my birthday, and I turned one year old. I had a wonderful day. I got to play outside with Crieff that morning, and then I got a birthday party! All my friends came; Auntie Marcia made me a birthday cake. It was bone-shaped and made with chicken livers, eggs, honey, molasses, and some other yummy stuff. The frosting was peanut butter and cream cheese with honey. Yummmmm. It had my name on top in Eukanuba dog-food nuggets. The humans brought treats for themselves, too.

We had a bone hunt. Our humans hid bone-shaped cookies under and around the agility equipment in the dog school. We each got one minute to find as many as we could. When we found something, it was collected in a basket—if the human could get to it before we ate it. Then the dog who had the most cookies in their basket won an extra prize, but we all got to keep our "found biscuits."

I even got birthday presents. I got a new tug-toy. I got a bone-shaped cookie with "Happy Birthday" on it from a dog bakery, a new neck scarf with dogs and "Happy Birthday" on it, and a new, fancy dog collar for my theatre wardrobe.

I like to go to places. Today, we would visit as Mrs. Gotrocks, the wealthy matron of the theatre, with her many jewels and chiffon scarves around her neck, cape, her sparkly little pillbox hat with the feathers in it, her "diamond"-studded glasses or some other outrageous pair of glasses. I have at least a dozen to choose from. I can go dressed to the hilt, or I can be dressed very casually, or anything in between. I had a wonderful birthday.

CHAPTER 9

POTPOURRI

Okay, so I am not a German Shepherd Dog. Okay, so I don't have a "slow" button. Okay, so I got blisters on my feet playing "run the fence" with Edin. Okay, so he stopped and rested, and he went slowly while I raced up and down. I still walk, anyway. Doesn't that count? Auntie Ann says I have to rest this week and let my feet heal. I don't even get to go to class! Can you believe that?

Yesterday was Mother's Day. So, Auntie Ann, Auntie Marcia, and I went to Auntie Ann's mother's house. I got to go since I was on paw rest because of my foot blisters and because I am a Border Collie who really hates being in a crate and, who, if left unattended in the house, somehow manages to get into trouble.

The trip was a great adventure. I had never met this person Auntie Marcia calls "Honey" (her grandmother). When we got there and I went into her backyard to potty, imagine my surprise to see a *cat*. It ran, and *boy!* I really wanted to chase it, but I was told to "Leave it!" So I did. Honey thought I was pretty. She said that I was bigger than she thought I would be. How would I be able to herd 300-pound sheep if I were scrawny?

My nose was going 100 miles a minute. There were so many different smells. *Wow!!!!* Her house was so different. There was not one dog smell in the whole house. Not one. I guess we keep all the dogs at our house. I wasn't uncomfortable there; it was just very different. I had to do down-stays. Auntie Ann and Auntie Marcia said it was good training for therapy work.

Okay, so I would rather be exploring, but it was okay. Auntie Marcia had gotten me a new toy that was supposedly indestructible—even for Border Collies. I had been chewing on it, and it was holding up. Everyone seemed pleased. I liked it. I thought it was a great toy. Everyone was happy about that. I had it in the car with me. I had the whole back seat to myself, and I could sit up and watch all the people do things. Sometimes you see dogs—and cats—in the other cars. I go nuts over seeing a cat. They can really run fast, and they climb trees, so, you can chase them up a tree. Now Auntie Ann says I have to take Inky lessons. I knew we had a kennel cat named "Inky," whom I had not yet met, but I don't know what "Inky practice" is. I guess I'll find out.

After the visit, and after I went out into the backyard to potty again, I looked, but the cat was gone. We loaded up in the car and left for home. But before we got home, we pulled off and went to *another* new place. We all went in, and again, there were so many new smells that my head was flooded! We walked down this long hall in this huge building, and one of the doors smelled like *Auntie Marcia*! She said this is where she comes each day when she is not home. Auntie Marcia said I could explore here. It was fascinating. There were lots and lots of people there, and, at the door, there was this really cute bone-shaped rug and *Surprise!* I smelled Beta and Gracie, two of my good friends from school! What had they been doing here? So many questions, but we had to leave. Auntie Marcia just had to get something from her room.

By then, I was a tired puppy, and, when I got home, it was good to see my bed. I guess you can have a pretty good time even if you have blisters on your feet and you are on paw rest. The questions I had would have to wait until tomorrow. Right then, I just had to sleep.

Next morning, I had my first "Inky lesson." *Oh, my goodness!* I just couldn't believe it! Richard brought Inky into the office and put her in a crate. Auntie Ann held me firmly in her lap, because I wanted to chase her. I remembered what Tess, Maggie, Reba, and Brownie told me: Cats have claws and can swat you, but Inky didn't even run. In fact, she was very nice. She kept rubbing up against the crate, and she let me get my nose right into her fur. I sniffed her for a good fifteen minutes. She sure doesn't smell like any dog I have ever smelled before. I'd just never smelled anything like her. She was just so interesting. I was just deciding that she could stay in our office in the crate when Auntie Ann told Auntie Marcia to let Inky out of the crate.

I didn't know exactly what that meant until the door swung open, and out walked Inky. I mean, she just strolled right out and right up to me and rubbed up against me! Can you imagine that? She walked right under my stomach, like tunneling. Can you imagine that? And then she strolled around the office. I, of course, followed her and tried to herd her, but she didn't do that very well, and then she jumped right onto the chair and peered down at me like she was the queen or something. Then, she jumped up onto the table, and I put my feet up on the chair to see her better. I thought about jumping up onto the table, but I was already face-to-face with her. She didn't like that much, and, out of the blue, she swatted me! I backed off. Well, it surprised me, and she has claws, but she was nice after that, like nothing had happened. She was pretty nice. I just never have been that close to a cat before.

What a lesson! Maybe I can get another "Inky lesson" soon.

We have these very good dog biscuits. They're just delicious. We seem to have a lot of them, but they are just so good that I get afraid that, someday, they just won't be here. Who knows? Maybe Auntie Ann will forget to buy some, or the guy will forget to deliver them, or they, heaven forbid, will stop making them. So, I hide them. I hide them everywhere. I also believe in sharing. I am generous, after all. I shared them with Crieff.

Now, I don't have to share with Rayne. She has her own biscuit bank under the cushion she sleeps on. It's sort of like the people who stuff their money in the mattress. I know she can't walk very well, so she has to keep them close. If you get too close to her Biscuit Bank, believe me, she will let you know. This normally mild-mannered dog will show her teeth and growl at you. I'm told there was a palomino horse on TV, named "Mr. Ed," who talked and showed his teeth a lot. Everyone calls Rayne "Mrs. Ed" when she gets that toothy look on her face. I think she is bored out of her mind and plays mind games with us. She is convincing; however, I am not going to be the one to push her. Crieff pushes her. I don't know how, but he gets away with it.

Sometimes I hide my biscuits in plain sight, on the stairs, on the floor. Sometimes I hide them on the chairs under the dining-room table, or in the flowerpots, on, under, or in the chair cushions, or on or under the coffee table. Sometimes I leave them as a surprise under people's pillows on the bed.

Last night, Uncle Roger left his swimming bag on the floor, and so, yep! He found it this morning, when he was in the locker room at the swimming pool. I bet he was the only person whose dog thought enough of him to tuck a snack into his swim bag for after swimming! He thought it was pretty funny. I put it way in the bottom. He showed Auntie Ann, and they both laughed.

Auntie Ann has discovered that I also love popcorn. She shares hers with me. Crieff and Rayne don't like popcorn.

CHAPTER 10

MY COUSINS

I have a cousin whose name is Jacques. He is a Standard Poodle, ten months old. He and his dad, Adam, came to visit us for two weeks. They wanted Auntie Ann to give them lessons, and boy! *We* did!

It was so much fun to have Jacques in the house with me. We played and played and played some more from morning to night, unless we were working or in class. I taught him how to play tug. He isn't very good at it. I taught him how to climb the stairs and how to come down the stairs. I taught him how to play "Shepherd Tag," like a German Shepherd Dog, like Crieff taught me. We watched Window View, which is better than TV because the screen is bigger and the stuff you are watching is real and in the front yard, so you may stand a chance of catching it when you go outside. I shared my cookies with him, and he shared his food with me. He wouldn't eat when he came, but I showed him his food was really good, so he learned to eat. I wasn't going to let good food go to waste! I'm Scottish. I was taught better.

We had a scare with him in Rayne's park. Crieff, Scotia, Jacques, and I were up there to play and run, and Ponder, a German Shepherd Dog, came up on the other side of the fence. It is so much fun to play run-the-fence with him, so we were all running the fence; we got into a scrum[11] and *pow*! Somehow Jacques got run over, and he came up limping. Auntie Ann was worried because of what had happened to Rayne, so she and Adam took Jacques to the vet for X-rays. We did find out he has excellent hips, and after a few days' rest, he was fine, but it certainly ended our play session. Rats.

Jacques hikes with his dad in the wilderness of Red Rock Canyon near Las Vegas, Nevada. Adam calls Jacques his "insurance policy." I think it's like golf being the "insurance policy" for Alec, Grace's brother-in-law.

I wish I could go hiking in the wilderness of Red Rock Canyon, but Auntie Ann says I have to learn to come when I am called first. I have trouble with that one. I have learned a lot at school, and I mind everything else but that one. I hear my name and head the other way. I don't know why. We're working on it. Auntie Ann says I will not be allowed off-leash outside unless I am in the training field, which is fenced, until I learn to come every time I am called. Meantime, every other dog here gets to run off-leash, even the baby puppies!

Speaking of the baby puppies—the orphaned ones, remember? They are so cute! I just love them, and I have become their babysitter and teacher. I am, of course, bigger than they are, so I have to get down low, so I don't scare them and so they can reach me.

---

11 See Miste's Vocabulary—Chapter 22

They climb on my head and hang on my tail. When I lie clear down, they jump on top of me and wrestle with me. Of course, I let them win. They think they have a death hold on my throat, but they aren't biting very hard at all. I wiggle and wriggle, and pretend they are really getting the better of me, and they just love it. When we walk out into the yard, they follow me, and I teach them how to go potty outside. At dog school, I teach them how to sit and be quiet sometimes and how to go to work when you should. I taught them how to traverse the A-frame, how to go through the long tunnels, how to do the chute, even though you can't see when you are in there, how to do the dog walk, and how to work the teeter-totter.

I have another cousin named "Bella." She is a Cavalier King Charles Spaniel. I have taught her lots of things, too. For example, I taught her how to save and hide her cookies. Now she hides them everywhere around her house, and the humans are always finding cookies everywhere. She loves to come here and stay when her humans are out of town.

Rayne, who knows *everything*, was right. I have my paws full.

I went to my second performance. I have a signature trick now, and everyone loves it. I back up ten or fifteen feet away from Auntie Marcia, Auntie Ann, or Jordan, and then I sit. Then they wave "Hello" to me, and I wave back with one paw. Everyone just loves it. Well, I did my trick and performed in a couple of the drills last Saturday, when, out of the blue, this woman walked up and said, "I want to see the Border Collie," and came straight for me. She had no dogs with her, but she smelled of dogs—lots and lots of them—and medicine. I knew she was not a member of our drill team, and none of the dogs whose scent she was carrying were anyone I knew. All the other people didn't smell like they had dogs at all, or only maybe one or two, so I knew they were the audience. I had only a split second to react. But I put it together! She was a dog-napper!!! Well, she wasn't going to get me!!! I growled at her, and my hair went up! I gave her my fiercest, most intense Collie eye. She backed off. Hah! I showed her. She wasn't going to take me to wherever she put those other dogs!

Well, later, I found out she was a veterinarian and a friend to the drill team. How was I supposed to know? I had never met a veterinarian outside the "vet's office." Auntie Ann understood and explained it, and now everyone understands. It was a mis-understanding. Guess I still have a lot to learn. Auntie Ann says the more I go to these things, the more I will learn to take things in stride and learn to read "my" people, and if they aren't afraid or upset, then I shouldn't worry, either. After that, I went up to adults and children, and everybody did just fine. I have to learn I cannot break "stays" to chase after balls and my friends before I can take my therapy-dog test. I don't quite have that down yet, but I'm learning. We go to class every night, and we are trying to get the puppies up there also, but sometimes that is hard. Even though the puppies get a bath every day, they get into stuff and get dirty or wet (for example, they climb into their water bucket) right before class. Mindin is the worst, because she has a long coat and doesn't dry as quickly.

Last night, Auntie Ann had a private lesson that ran right up to class time. I needed to help with that. I had been outside all day, playing with Crieff and Edin (short for Edinburgh) . . . in a fenced run, of course . . . and I was exhausted. Everyone was chuckling that a Border Collie was worn out. So, I showed them. I bounced up this morning and was rarin' to go again—after cuddle practice, of course. I hopped on the bed, and Auntie Ann rubbed my tummy and gave me a massage. I used to allow that for ten seconds or less. Now I am up to three to five minutes, depending on how tired I am at the time. Sometimes, now, I even come and ask if I can have a lesson. I never used to do that. I always gave quick kisses, but now I stay a lot longer. I am now addicted to cuddle time.

CHAPTER 11

LAUREN'S TALENT SHOW

It was nearly midnight when the phone woke us all up. It was Clark, Auntie Ann's son. They had recently moved from Las Vegas to St. Louis, and Lauren, Auntie Ann's granddaughter, had started a new school. The teacher had announced their school was going to have a talent show. The teacher divided the class into two groups. The boys were on one side and the girls on the other, planning their talent acts. Lauren went to the girls' side and was greeted with, "We don't want you!" Lauren came home in tears. She wanted to participate in the talent show, but these girls were not going to let her into their group. She needed a talent, and, so, naturally, they thought of *me*! I was so excited. I was so proud that everyone thought I had learned enough to be able to do this. Of course, *I* knew I could, but I wasn't sure that my humans knew it!

Immediately, we began practicing the routine Auntie Marcia and Auntie Ann wrote. I love kids, but—and it's not their fault—they are very inconsistent with their signals. It's all right for you to tell me I'm smart and that I should be able to figure it out. Really? *You* try to get it when your short person doesn't know the routine and gets the signals all mixed up as well! I tried to tell her, but she either didn't understand me or didn't *want* to understand me. Maybe she thought I was some kind of machine . . . just punch all the buttons. I tried. I honestly tried. But I could feel myself getting more and more frustrated. I just couldn't do it. I didn't want to make a fuss, but I just couldn't, and, frankly, I didn't want to do it anymore. Besides, tempers were getting short, and I absolutely dread conflict.

So, when tempers started flaring again, I left the floor and got a drink. Then I flopped on the floor, away from the dancing area, and I wouldn't get up. I cannot stand arguing, and I could feel gloom descending. I just wanted to disappear. Lauren, Auntie Marcia, and Auntie Ann practiced without me, and, finally, Lauren and her family went home. The show would be on the upcoming Tuesday, and it was Sunday already. There was no more time to practice. Lauren was upset now and not sure that I would work for her, and since I was refusing to work anymore, I was miserable, but at the same time, I was not *Superdog*. If Lauren wanted me to work, then she should have given me the correct signals.

On Tuesday, it was a two-hour ride to Lauren's school. We pulled into a McDonald's. I love McDonald's chicken strips. They are my very favorite. I know all the McDonald's arches and point them all out to Auntie Ann in case she didn't see them. Maybe she would stop by and maybe get some chicken strips? Well, this day, Uncle Roger bought two boxes. My mouth started watering, and in my mind, I was already tasting that delicious chicken with just the perfect smell and flavor. I could picture my mouth stuffed with that wonderful stuff . . . the flavor rolling across my tongue and traveling to my brain. What a wonderful day this was!

Auntie Ann put one of the boxes in her purse and then lifted a big piece of chicken out of the other box. I never took my eyes off that irresistible piece of sheer joy. Auntie Ann's fingers raised the chicken out of the box, and I thought, *Here it comes!* My mouth opened with anticipation—and Auntie Ann handed it to Uncle Roger! Well, that was okay. He'd paid for them. He should get the first piece. There were more. I would get the next piece. Sharing was good. Now, Uncle Roger will know how good they are and will want to stop in often. Well, one can dream.

Oh, no! Auntie Ann was not giving me that next piece, either. She was eating it herself, and she wasn't even looking at me! I barked—no response! I put on my pleading look—actually, I didn't *have* to put it on because *I was actually pleading*. Auntie Ann and Uncle Roger ate most of the chicken strips right in front of me. The scent saturated the air in the car. I was drooling uncontrollably. Then Auntie Ann put the last two pieces in her purse, along with with the other box. Uncle Roger started the car, and we drove on.

What was going on here? They knew how much I loved those, and they didn't give me even one—not even a *piece* of one! Why? What did I do? I finally lay down in the back seat. Who cared where we were going or what we were or weren't doing? This wasn't a wonderful day. This was an awful, miserable, mean day. I didn't care anymore.

We weren't in the car very long when we turned into a parking lot. It looked like a school. There were lots of kids playing on a playground at the back. Suddenly, Lauren appeared and opened the car door to the back seat. It's hard to explain what happened next. All of a sudden, I realized how important I was to Lauren. I realized how important the routine we had been practicing was to her and the whole family. Auntie Ann gave Lauren the chicken strips to put into her treat pouch—*all of them*: the two left over *and* the other whole box! Lauren immediately gave me some pieces. My heart jumped for joy. I was ready!

We went into the gym. There was a stage at one end. We went through a door at one end beside the stage. We went through another door that led to some stairs, which led to a room beside the stage . . . like a waiting room where we could stay until it came time for our routine. You could hear the kids coming in, and the noise volume in the gym got louder and louder. It kinda hurt my ears, but I could handle it. I just had to concentrate on what I was supposed to be doing.

The principal stepped out of the curtains at the side of the stage where we were waiting. As she walked to the front center of the stage, the kids fell silent. She opened the show and introduced "Miss Susan," who was in charge of the whole show. The wait was draggy, but Lauren gave me a bite of chicken strip every few minutes, so that was fine. I kept thinking about everything. I could see how important this was to my Lauren, and I could see how I could really help.

One of the acts involved the girls, who were now not speaking to Lauren. They were the ones who wouldn't let Lauren join their group. They still weren't including her. I could feel their hostility. I could also feel Lauren's hurt. Some other kids began to realize something was going on, and they moved away from Lauren, not wanting to be alienated themselves but not quite understanding what the problem was. I snuggled into Lauren to focus her on our job—focus her on what we had to do, and never mind anyone else.

So, when Miss Susan introduced us, I pranced onto that stage with Lauren with as much flair as I could muster.

Our music started. I did not only the tricks and moves in the drill but also some new, extra ones. The crowd cheered and squealed with delight. They loved us. Lauren beamed. She was my pay. I was happy.

The performance went flawlessly! When we came off the stage, the short people (as I call kids) all crowded around, wanting to pet me and peppering Lauren with questions about where I came from and how she got me to do what she wanted me to do. It was wonderful. Even the uppity girls came over and joined the crowd with smiles on their faces. I found out I was the first dog *ever* to perform in their school. *Wow! Me!* A little dog from Scotland coming to this wonderful country and being a first? *Wow!* I tried to calm my excitement and act cool, calm, and collected, even if I didn't quite feel that way!

CHAPTER 12

AUNTIE MARCIA'S SCHOOL

My usual day runs something like this:

I get up, and the first thing is snuggle time. I used to call it snuggle *practice*, however, I don't need the practice anymore. I am *addicted* to it. I have to have my snuggle time before I do anything else. Then I go out to potty and eat breakfast. Then I find Auntie Ann again and get another snuggle. I have come to realize snuggles are one of the most important times of the day.

The middle of the day is anyone's guess. You never know what we will be doing.

Some days, we have lessons at the dog-training building; sometimes we have to go someplace to give a performance, and sometimes we have to stay home and work on projects. Sometimes I have to exercise the puppies, who are growing and are running very fast—not as fast me, though. The puppies are almost as tall as I am now. I think of all the lonely days I spent in the crate when

Grace was dying. I know it wasn't anyone's fault. They couldn't help it, but it sure hurt—the whole thing just hurt. Now, every day, we do stuff. We do stuff all day and into the night. I fall into bed at night to sleep quickly, so that I can get up in the morning to go again. There isn't a lonely day here. There just isn't time.

Guess *what*! Kenzie made me my first new clothes![12] I was wearing German Shepherd Dog hand-me-downs and borrowed clothes. They were okay, I guess, and I was grateful that at least I didn't feel left out, but they were frequently too big.

I just didn't know that having your own new clothes would feel so good. Everyone says I look just adorable in them. They are technically for the "Circus in the Park" show we will do this summer with the thirty-one-piece circus band, so I can clown around with my team. I am wondering what that will be like. I like new things, mostly, but I have heard mixed reports. I hear it will take some getting used to. It will be quite an experience, I hear. I guess the band is quite loud, and, most of the time, we are right next to them.

My new clothes are very pretty on me. Soft colors set off my black-and-white coat. Uncle Roger will try to find time to put the picture of me in my new clothes on the webpage. Thank you, Kenzie. I am so excited, because now, I have a cute trick—I back up, sit, and wave. Everyone loves it. Now, I have new clothes to perform it in.

We got all washed and dressed up in our themes for the month, called Circus in the Park. My wardrobe had to expand. At Christmas, for example, we wear colorful neck ruffles, and we get into all sorts of stuff in January. In February, it's huge, heart-shaped glasses, which made us look pretty funny. March brought

---

12 See Miste's Vocabulary, Chapter 22

squiggly horns on the head; April brought out the rain gear; in May, I wore a white straw hat with flowers in the headband. I looked positively smashing! We had our pictures taken; the pictures were put on the bookmarks for each month, and we handed them out to the kids, who had to earn the right to read to us. When the short people finish their turn to read, they receive a bookmark with a picture of the dog they read to on it. We make new bookmarks each month. They became collector's items.

On May 28th, we are going to Auntie Marcia's school for a performance. I hear *that* is loud as well. I hear we are treated like rock stars, whatever those are. Rayne, who knows *everything*, says the kids shout a lot, cheering us on because they love us so much. The honor of performing with the drill team has always gone to Auntie Marcia's class because she brings the drill team to school, and it is *her* drill team, after all. Marcia generously includes the other second-graders. The kids come into the ring. The short people line up and spread their legs so we can all tunnel under them. Then they sit in a line on the floor, and we all jump their legs. Then we pick a few children to get down on their hands and knees, and we have some of the little dogs crawl under them.

So, it's good that I will have my new clothes for that show as well. Everyone is very pleased that I don't pull my leg ruffles off. Not me! You can say I'm thrilled to be wearing clothes—kind of like Dobby, the house elf in *Harry Potter*. I have my white straw hat with the pretty flowers and ribbons around the band. I also have a neck ruffle to match my leg ruffles, which are made with very cheerful material, all matching the flowers in the hat.

Friday (May 28th) was my kind of day! I knew the minute we got up that we were going someplace. I didn't know where, but I *was ready!* Well, I thought I was, but I had to go out and potty, and then we had to finish packing the car, and I had to get my special tartan scarf on, leashes on, potty again, and finally, Crieff, Scotia, and I got into the car.

I love the car. I love riding shotgun in front, where you can see everything going by. It goes by so fast—my brain has trouble cramming it all in! I love it! It is such a challenge! However, Richard proceeded to get into my front seat. Crieff didn't care. He just plopped down in the back seat and settled in for a nap. I will never understand how anyone could nap at a time like this. Scotia likes to ride in the crate in the back because she doesn't like being pushed off the back seat by Crieff. Crieff learned from Rayne (the one who knows *everything*) that, if you immediately get into the car and lie down next to the back of the seat, anyone else who gets in gets only what is left over. It usually doesn't affect me because I ride in the front seat anyway, but Scotia prefers to have her own compartment in the back, so she has all the room she wants and doesn't have to argue about it. Arguing always gets us into trouble.

So, I had to put my feet on the console between Auntie Ann and Richard, and watch out the front window. If Crieff was missing all this, well, *that's his tough luck*. What a ride! We had to keep track of Auntie Marcia's car, in front of us, and Uncle Roger's car, behind us. I heard we were going to Auntie Marcia's school. I had been there once before, a few weeks before. Now I would have the whole family there!!!

We pulled around back. I had never been in the back of the school building, so that was interesting, and then this short person came out with a ball. That was it! We had come to play *ball*. But no, Auntie Ann would not let me out of the car. Then I saw my friend EmmyLu (a Jack Russell Terrier) come around the corner! Right after her came my friends Wendy (a Sheltie) and Sophie (a

Cocker Spaniel/Poodle mix), and then Zeke (a chocolate Lab), Laverne (a German Shepherd mix), and Shirley (a hound mix), and I knew then we were here to give a performance!

I wanted to go in, but we had to wait until all the equipment was in, as well as the crates for Scotia and Crieff. I was not in a crate. I get to stay with Auntie Ann. I have finally, I think, taught them that this is where I belong. It has taken me a while. Sometimes, I have had to correct them very loudly and persistently. I was glad they realized that, today, we were in public. They would have been embarrassed if I'd had to correct them in public, which, I am proud to say, they *know* I would have done. I know, sometimes my corrections give Crieff and Rayne a headache, but if you don't correct these humans immediately and persistently, they just don't learn. Sometimes I can correct with some gurgling and whining sounds; sometimes an "Arff" will do, but sometimes I have to give my loudest, most demanding bark, complete with nasty bark and half-growl. It is really a case of my bark being a whole lot worse than my bite. I try very hard to do what they ask, but, sometimes, you just have to put your paw down.

Finally, it was our turn to go in. My nose was everywhere—so much to analyze and process! More of the team started arriving: Gordon, a huge Chesapeake Bay Retriever; the Bichons—Bebe and Tooter; Chip, the Chihuahua; Kasey, the Beagle mix; Bernard, the Puggle; Gracie, the German Shepherd mix; Brownie, the all-American-who-knows-what; Gabe, a German Shepherd Dog; Lily, a French Bulldog; Ricky, a Havanese puppy who has a crush on me; Lucy, a Beagle; Maggie, a yellow Lab; Yukon, a huge, gorgeous Malamute; Sierra, a black Lab; Toby, a chocolate Lab; and Beta, an Australian Cattle Dog. Also, Cody, a Sheltie, and Ellie, a German Shepherd Dog, were there.

The school bells were ringing, and everyone was rushing here and there, getting everything set up and dogs hitched to their wagons. I am learning how to pull a wagon, but I'm not good enough yet to pull one in a show.

But then all these short people started filing into the gym (that is where we were), and the noise got louder and *louder*. I know my eyes got bigger and *bigger*. But then I figured they were all on the other side of the ring gates, so that was not bad.

The show went on, and I stayed by Auntie Ann. I did a drill with Jordan while Sierra rested. It was a little disconcerting when I had to get next to the ring gates, where the screaming, cheering mob was, but I managed. I was even steady when Auntie Ann had to put me on a *sit-stay* in the second-grade drill while the second-graders skipped around me, but, *then,* they all slowed down, and several of them started touching me—*all at once!* I jumped out of my skin and right into Auntie Ann's arms, which were not ready to catch me! *Touching wasn't part of the plan*—not *my* plan anyway! I guess Auntie Marcia's class wanted to meet me, and they were upset they didn't get to, but I needed recovery time. Then, I went with Auntie Ann to the ring gate, and she put some of my very favorite treats into the kids' hands, and she knew I could not resist them. I took them with trepidation, to say the least.

At last, we packed up and left for home. I was glad to get in the car again but too tired to watch out the front window. There was hardly enough room on the seat because Crieff was hogging it all. I was beginning to think that Scotia had the right idea, and I was wishing I had a crate. *What am I saying?* I *hate* crates! Still . . .

I climbed into the back, but Auntie Ann said I couldn't stay there because there was a lot of traffic, with starting and stopping, and she was afraid the load would shift or I would slip and get a leg stuck, so I crowded onto this (maybe big-enough), spot next to Crieff. It wasn't long before we were home again. I surely wouldn't want the trip to have lasted any longer.

Thinking back about the show at Auntie Marcia's school, I saw that I have a lot to learn. I watched my friends and saw how calm they were. I know I can do it, too. I just have to learn. Auntie Ann, Uncle Roger, Auntie Marcia, Jordan, and all my other friends are helping me. How could I possibly fail?

A few days later, we all—Auntie Marcia, Richard, Auntie Ann, and I—went out to Auntie Marcia's school. We helped her pack up her room for the summer—about seven weeks. We will have to come back in seven weeks to put Auntie Marcia's classroom all back together. In the meantime, we had to take down the fabric on the bulletin boards, curtains, chair covers, pillows, and all sorts of things to take home, wash, and bring them back. We have cubbies and shelves to paint and bring back, and we have to sort all the books into different categories, like Civil War, Revolutionary War, Science, Biographies, Fairy Tales, Poetry, Arts and Crafts, Tall Tales, Folk Tales, and there is even a whole basket for dogs! Then there are all these things called "math manipulatives." I have no idea what those are. We don't use them in the "Reading to Rover" program.[13]

When we are out like this, of course, all of us workers need lunch, so Auntie Ann gets me a grilled burger (that's hip American talk for "hamburger"). Sometimes I get crackers or other treats with my burger, like chips. Oh, that's Scottish for what Americans call "French fries."

---

13 See Miste's Vocabulary, Chapter 22

CHAPTER 13

TDI TEST

I knew something was up last night when I had to take a bath at 9 o'clock! I had trouble sleeping after that, wondering what was up. Then, this morning, we packed up the car with directions and a list of stuff. *We never make a list unless it is someplace far away or a drill-team performance. What?* I wondered. Well, we drove miles and finally arrived at this place with all these dogs, but none of them were my drill-team friends! What is this?!!! What is going on here? Where are you, my friends?

Well, I got out to potty, and I couldn't believe all the dogs that had been there. There were at least thousands. My nose was working as fast as I could intake the material. Then we walked inside, and there were dogs all over the place! I was on my buckle collar so I could pull really hard, and Auntie Ann pulled really hard back. She kept saying "Easy," I guess, but I didn't really hear her because I had all this other information I *had* to process. We got inside and went downstairs in an elevator, and there were more dogs down there! I heard someone say this was a dog museum, a place all about all kinds of dogs.

Auntie Marcia left Scotia on a *down/stay* next to me and left to go find the restroom. This was such a cool place. It—I mean the *whole* place—is about us! They really love us! What a place to show off and play! So, I did. I invited Scotia to play, and she told me that her mama, Auntie Marcia, told her to down/stay, and *that* was what she was going to do! I thought if I just convinced her that she really didn't have to do that, we could have a really fun time. Then Auntie Ann's hand took hold of my collar, gave it a twist, and told me to *Stop it!* in unmistakable terms, and she didn't even say a word. How can humans do that? I got the very clear and very strong message. I got it loud and clear.

Auntie Marcia returned and told Auntie Ann there was a large room next door that she might want to use for a few minutes. I was eager to go see it as well, and when we got there, my nose went to the floor, benches, and wherever else it could go. I had *never* smelled so many dogs in my life! I was so busy smelling that I swear I did not hear Auntie Ann tell me several times to "Leave it!" But I sure felt that hand grab me by the back of the collar, quickly and forcefully plunk me on my bottom, and tell me, *"We're working!"* There were several fast and quickly reinforced commands after that, and I got the message. We were here to work, and I was expected to listen and follow directions. So, I decided I would try.

Oh, my goodness! It was a *test*, a test over all the stuff we had been learning at school. This was no play session. The evaluator's name was Virginia. We were here for the toughest test of my life! I didn't know these people, these dogs, or this place, and I had to remember all this stuff I was supposed to have learned! I wished

I had paid more attention in class. We had to stay in a row, next to dogs and people that Scotia and I did not know. There was this one nervous-nelly, a Poodle-Irish Setter mix, whining about how our owners were going to leave us there for sure, and then she kept jumping up and bucking on the leash. I admit I was a little worried. I wanted to find my humans. I figured if I stayed, it was the safest thing to do. Well, anyway, that's what Scotia said. I thought about that, and I didn't see a choice that was better.

After what seemed like an eternity, Auntie Marcia and Auntie Ann came back. It was a relief. Then, they put treats in one person's hands, and we were supposed to "Leave it" (which means *Don't take the treat*). That usually was very hard, because our humans use chicken livers and other wonderful treats, but today they had some treats I had tried before and didn't like. So, this was an easy test for me. The whole test seemed endless to me. Then we had to wait to see if we'd passed or flunked. To me, it took forever! Finally, came the announcement: *I passed!* But then, I had to turn right around and take the test again with Auntie Marcia. No one else had to do that. I didn't see why I had to, but I passed again, and then I got the drift. Now, I am qualified to visit with both Auntie Ann and Auntie Marcia. I passed, and, of course, Scotia passed. There was never any question about her.

We walked around the museum a little and wowed some of the visitors with our *sit/stays* and *down/stays* in different pictorial scenes for photos. It was not really a difficult thing, but I guess they don't have dogs who go to school, because they were certainly impressed with me and Scotia. It sure made me feel good, and I began to recognize that following directions can be really fun. So, I was on my almost-very-good behavior when we finished the visit in the museum's gift shop.

We had just made it to the car to come home when a terrible rainstorm hit, and I got to play "Chase the Windshield Wipers" for a few minutes! *Wheeeeee!* We were back in our own car; no one could see us, and everyone was gone anyway . . . mostly. Those windshield wipers drove me wild. I was determined to catch them. I just *had* to catch them. I guess I didn't pay attention to where my feet went. I guess I didn't listen to what my Aunties Ann and Marcia were saying: "No!"—ordering me to stop. I guess I was a bit of a whirling dervish. Auntie Ann and Auntie Marcia were struggling to control me. Scotia was looking mortified, and Auntie Ann and Auntie Marcia were looking over their shoulders, obviously praying no one recognized me or them, either. Auntie Ann kept saying that, if they recognized us, they might revoke our passing the test.

Why is everyone so uptight? Loosen up, folks. I guess I had calmed down enough, and we finally left there—and this is the very best part: Even after my apparent misbehavior, Aunties Ann and Marcia took Scotia and me through the Steak and Shake drive-through and got us ice cream and steakburgers! Boy! Did those ever hit the spot! So much so, they drove through again and got us a second steakburger! Steak and Shake has become my favorite spot.

Guess what! *I passed!* I know I told you already, but *I passed.* In fact, I passed *two* tests: my CGC (Canine Good Citizen) and my TDI (Therapy Dogs International). Auntie Ann has to send in my paperwork, picture, vet health form, and other information, but that should all go through. We will be getting it all together this week. Once I get all that back—*and* my official badge—I can start visiting, and my work with the drill team will go toward other, more-advanced therapy-dog titles. I will also get an official certificate and title from the American Kennel Club for passing my CGC—Canine Good Citizen—test.

I think Mom (Grace) would have been proud of me. Do you think so? I know I still have a lot to learn, but *Look out, world! Here I come!*

I think I got in a little trouble yesterday for not behaving quite as well in public as Auntie Ann wanted. I passed two tests. I don't see a problem myself, but I am getting the idea that Auntie Ann's standards are higher, and she is not lowering them. I guess I shouldn't have pulled quite as hard or sniffed . . . now I am getting corrected . . . I should have *stopped* sniffing when I was told to "Stop sniffing." (What I would like to know is: how are we to gather all that information if we don't sniff?) Uh, oh. She heard me. She said that was information I didn't need to know! But, I *wanted* to know it. (Sigh.) I guess I have a lot to learn. That's okay. That stop at Steak and Shake was worth it, and if you have to behave to get to go, then I will try to learn to behave. Besides, I want to see what the rest of you guys do and where you go! I'm ready to go anywhere. . . .

Two weeks later, I got my CGC certificate and my ID for passing the TDI tests in the mail. I am now official! I am a card-carrying therapy dog! I can now go on official visits! I have a new red scarf and a tag that I have to wear on my collar that identifies me as an official therapy dog. My ID card has my picture on it. Now I can go into hospitals, nursing homes, schools, preschools, the library, just all over.

You might think that my schooling is complete, but it isn't. Auntie Ann says it has only just begun! This fall, I have to pass another test. It is called a "temperament test." I will have to start studying for that when Auntie Ann and Uncle Roger get back from Scotland.

Meantime, my obedience lessons will continue; my agility lessons and my drill-team lessons (we practiced tunneling under other people's legs today, for example; I always pop out too soon and miss the rest of the circle . . . oops!). Then there are my cuddle lessons, manners lessons, socialization lessons, and my water lessons (I am taking hose and tubs right now), and, of course, there is always recess! At recess, I love to herd the big red ball all over Rayne's Park. Rayne's Park is our playground at school. It has an outdoor dog walk, a huge tunnel, weave polls, jumps, a log A-frame, and a really fun dog slide. We also play "Keep Away." I usually win that. I'm an expert at faking out the opponent and stealing the toy from him or her. Crieff is catching on to my tricks, however, and, sometimes, he can get the toy away from me. "Tug of War" is my favorite game of all. Sometimes, I have to shove the tug toy into somebody else's mouth to get them to play tug with me because I am so good at it; like I said, I usually win! I think they think, "What's the use?" but I keep trying to tell them that the only way for them to get better is to practice, and I am just the one to do that with them!

I have to sign off for now. We have a thunderstorm going, and I have to keep everyone in line and tell them all about it.

CHAPTER 14

MISTE AND THE STORM

I can usually tell when we are going someplace by what Auntie Ann puts on to wear. She has a special uniform she puts on when we are going to perform someplace. If we are going someplace else, like Auntie Ann's mom's house (Auntie Marcia's grandmother), then I can tell by how much they are loading into the car. I am the last thing to get loaded!

Saturday, June 19th was a day for performing. It was exciting because the car was full of the ring gates, first-aid kits, emergency stuff, extra water, water bowls for Scotia and me, and our costumes for the show. Auntie Marcia sat in my seat up in front. I have not been able to convince her that she should sit in the back so I can ride shotgun. However, I put my feet on the console between Auntie Ann, who was driving, and Auntie Marcia, so I could see where we were going and also make sure the road was clear of *rabbits*! Why, I had to scare one off the driveway before we even left the property!!!

Scotia was riding in her compartment in the back. She says I step all over her in the back seat, but *I* say *she* doesn't get out of the way. This performance was about an hour and a half away from home, but the road was clear of rabbits all the way. It's a lot of work watching for rabbits, but someone has to do it.

Our performance for the Cancer Society benefit was to start at 2 p.m. We were supposed to perform, and then they were going to charge people to have us teach them how to do a musical drill. All of that money would also go to the Cancer Society. Well, we got there at 1 p.m. to set up the ring gates and get the crates for us out and set up, the jam box for the music, the flow sheets (a kind of map of who does what when), and the water bowls, water, costumes, chairs, tent, and all the other stuff we need.

We had just pulled up when the lady in charge asked us to set up as soon as possible because a large storm was coming out of Kansas City (further west than we were), and they were closing down at 2 p.m. Auntie Ann said to skip everything—just take the jam box, a chair for her, and the music, and we would leave the rest of the stuff in the car. We were performing in five minutes. We did four drills, but we were packing up before the fourth drill was finished because the sky had turned a very angry, dark blue-purple. As the team was coming off, all of a sudden, and I mean *all of a sudden,* the 70-mile-an-hour wind hit.

The wind picked up the dog crates and started rolling them around and into a fence. Everyone was grabbing everything they could get their hands on and running for the car. I was pulling Auntie Ann as hard as I could. I looked over my shoulder and wondered what was going on. It was a little scary, but I was trying to act calm. Scotia acted calm, although I noticed she didn't waste any time jumping into the car, and neither did I! Auntie Marcia and

Auntie Ann were helping everybody get loaded up, and the wind was fierce. Everything was flying by. A hamburger bun went flying by, and Toby, a Labrador Retriever, jumped up and caught it right out of midair! He wolfed it down. I certainly was not interested in eating at that time! My friend Chip, who is a Chihuahua, was in his crate, as his person, Robin, was putting things in her car when the wind picked up Chip—crate and all—and flung them through the air. Everybody grabbed for the crate and caught it. Chip was safe for the moment.

Kalee is a German Shepherd Dog on our drill team. About that time, Sarah, Kalee's mom, drove up and was shouting at us, "The radio just said to take cover immediately in a building."

Auntie Ann called back, "Which building—where?" There were no buildings around there, and the school was locked! We were still getting everyone's car loaded, and everyone was rushing and running back and forth. I just kept very still in my back seat in the car. The wind was blowing everything through the air: paper cups, straws, food, paper, and dust. Then everyone was in their cars, and Sarah pulled out. Kassidy—with EmmyLu, a Jack Russell Terrier, and Toby—was next, then Celia with Halle, an All-American, and we pulled out right behind them. I heard Auntie Ann say she was going wherever they were. In a couple of blocks, it became evident they were running for home, and so were we!

We got out on the highway, and the torrential rains began. I just got very quiet and let Auntie Marcia and Auntie Ann concentrate on the road. They both had their eyes on the road and the traffic. It took both of them to navigate the trip.

Finally, we pulled onto Interstate 70 and were hoping to outrun the storm. A loud pop scared us. It came from the back of the van. Auntie Marcia said an umbrella had popped open. Auntie Ann told

Auntie Marcia to ignore the umbrella, even though it was blocking some of the rear window. Both of them needed to pay attention to the highway, the storm, and the traffic. The storm appeared to be traveling right along with us. Auntie Marcia called Uncle Roger and asked him to look at the radar. He told us we would be in the storm for a little while. Well, we were in it all the way home! It didn't seem like *a little while* to us!

It was an interesting performance, however. We were supposed to start at 2 p.m., and we were finished at 1:30 p.m.! The storm was so bad, I guess it scared time backward!

CHAPTER 15

KING'S STORY

It sure gets hot here!

We were out in Rayne's Park. I got hot. Auntie Ann says it's because I'm running all the time! Well, it's fun to run in this huge, mowed field with the wind in your face, especially if there are others out there to *herd*! I love to herd the big, huge red ball, too. It needs it, because it is unruly and undisciplined. It never goes where I tell it to go!

Anyway, I got hot, so I got a drink out of the big, black bucket. Then I remembered that Crieff puts his feet in the water bucket when he drinks, so I decided to put my feet in the bucket. Well, that felt really good to my feet and legs, so I tried to get my back feet in as well. I just couldn't quite fit. I tried to stand on my head, but that didn't work, either! Everyone was laughing at me.

Soooo, Auntie Ann bought me a big metal tub. It's like a big washtub. Last night, I tried it out! It just fits me! I could get my whole self in it! I could twirl and spin and splash and jump in and out and swish my head under water! Swishing your head under water is the most fun! Everyone was laughing with me, and we were all having a wonderful time. I think I may be getting an even bigger tub. Kalee got one, and she didn't like it, so her mother may bring it over to us! Meanwhile, the big washtub is just wonderful!

It was another hot day, and we all had to come in to get the air conditioning. We could not go anywhere in the car because it would be too hot immediately if we stopped someplace. So, we all settled in and asked Rayne to tell us another story. This day, she told us a story about King.

"At the time, Auntie Ann lived with her widowed mother, had a job, and was engaged to be married. Across the street lived a couple who both worked full-time. They had a three-year-old German Shepherd Dog named King. Auntie Ann had made friends with King.

"There were no leash laws then, and everyone let their dogs run loose. Since King's owners were gone about fifteen hours a day, King ran loose about fifteen hours a day and had a bad reputation in the neighborhood. He had killed more than thirty cats and bitten three people.

"At this time, the man, Mr. Fisher, accepted what he considered his dream job in another state, and they were going to move there. The Fishers also owned a lot of investment property in town here, which they were now planning to sell if the job worked out as they expected it would. Over the next couple of weeks, the Fishers learned property was at a premium, and they were not able to find rental property that would allow dogs or a suitable house to buy at the new location. Mr. Fisher was expected at work shortly.

"Auntie Ann's widowed mother had agreed to buy a duplex from Mr. Fisher as an investment. She already owned some other rental properties in town. They had settled on a price and were working through the details of finalizing the agreement, so, when he appeared at the door one evening, she thought he was there to discuss that business. However, he had another proposition for her to consider. He explained their situation and said they needed a home for King. He said he could see how much Auntie Ann liked King and how much King liked her, and if Auntie Ann could take the dog, he would take five thousand dollars off the price of the duplex and pay to have all the papers changed and filed. In those olden days, five thousand dollars was a lot of money. Auntie Ann's mother agreed to the deal. King would move into the garage.

"When the time came for King to be fed, Auntie Ann was warned by Mr. Fisher to put his pan of food down and leave the room, or he would bite her. Do not leave him in a car by himself, or he will tear it apart. Don't push him by insisting he mind you, or he will bite you. He hates cats. (Well, everyone knew that was true!) And sooooo, life with King began.

"Auntie Ann spent time with him, playing "Keep Away," throwing balls, and then chasing him when he got them. She also started sitting in the same room when he ate. As he got less upset with that, she moved in closer, and, eventually, she sat with the pan in her lap as he ate. Gradually, she started working on his head and with his brain. In a year's time, she had him eating from her hand, had cats sleeping on top of him, and had his first title with AKC obedience. He had learned to mind Auntie Ann; he knew she would put him away and stop the lessons if he didn't mind her. For their formal lessons, he went to work with Auntie Ann and stayed in the car in a parking lot about a block away from Auntie Ann's work. Auntie Ann worked as a reporter for a radio and television station. While he stayed in the car during the day, Auntie Ann paid the parking lot attendant to walk him and give him drinks every hour. She herself checked on him during her lunch hour. Of course, they didn't do this in the summer because it was too hot.

"Once a week, after work, they drove to another part of the city and went to dog classes for German Shepherd Dogs. This was in a park between two four-lane boulevards. There were 100 German Shepherd Dogs, taking various levels of lessons in this park. The dogs were broken down into classes of ten each. The dogs worked their way up from the Beginning level, to Show levels, and up to a Utility level. King had worked himself up to the fourth level and had finished showing and obtaining his CD (Companion Dog) title with the American Kennel Club and some lovely blue ribbons to go with it. He was now starting on his Open title exercises for the next AKC title. He no longer killed cats and, in fact, would let cats crawl all over him and sleep on top of him. In fact, he came to really like cats and understand they were littler than him and needed to be addressed in a gentle way, and they were not rabbits or squirrels, which were okay to chase all he wanted. What a transformation he had made!

"One night at class, there was another German Shepherd Dog and his master sitting to the left of Auntie Ann and King, in a line to do some *sit-stays*. All of a sudden, this German Shepherd Dog leapt into the air in front of his master, straight at Auntie Ann's face. It all happened so fast . . . as he flew over the top of King, who was sitting at Auntie Ann's left side, King went straight up and grabbed this aggressive stranger by the underbelly. Auntie

Ann suddenly found herself on the ground with two ninety-pound dogs fighting on top of her. The instructor for the class was yelling "Help! Fight!" to the other nine instructors in the park, and all of them started to struggle with the two fighting male German Shepherd Dogs!

"Finally, they got the two separated and Auntie Ann back on her feet. Both dogs were bleeding from multiple puncture wounds and torn flesh. Both needed to go to the vet's office to get stitches. It was declared to be entirely the other dog's fault. Additionally, the dog had done this before to other dogs and people. The dog's owner paid for all of King's vet bills. Auntie Ann was fearful this would increase King's level of aggression, but it didn't seem to affect him in that way. She was grateful for the protection he gave her.

"Unfortunately, as wonderful as it was that King had learned all these things this year, Mr. Fisher had sold all his real-estate holdings in the area, and his dream job was going very well. They still had not been able to find housing to accommodate a dog, and anyway, according to the "deal" they had made, King belonged to Auntie Ann anyway. And so it was. Mr. Fisher left the area for good.

"As soon as he left, Auntie Ann's mother announced Auntie Ann was now to get rid of King. She didn't care how—just get rid of him, or she would. Auntie Ann pointed out all they had accomplished, but that didn't matter. Begging and pleading met the same admonition: King had to go, period. Privately, Auntie Ann cried and grieved. Auntie Ann tried to look at the situation from her mother's point of view; her mother was a widow. Dogs took time and work. They cost money for shots, food, and care (but Auntie Ann already paid for all that). Additionally, she took care of her little brother's German Shepherd Dog, who had no training. She also did quite a bit of work around the house, painting, laying tile, staining, and hanging shutters, besides housecleaning, dishes, and laundry. Still, this was her family, so, as told, Auntie Ann put an ad in the newspaper advertising King. She wanted some control over who got him, so she put her number at work in the ad. She wanted someone who would work with him and love him. A man called and asked lots of questions. He ended his line of questioning with an I-don't-believe-you attitude and a sneering question: 'Well, if he is so good, why are you getting rid of him?' Those words and that attitude cut deeply into Auntie Ann's heart and to the core of her being. She burst into tears and said tersely as she slammed down the phone, 'I'm *not!*'"

"Everything was flooding into her head now. When Auntie Ann was an early teen, the family had a young German Shepherd Dog named Ricky. It was the same Ricky who had gotten trapped in the snowstorm. The family had gone to visit relatives who lived on a farm. Ricky and Auntie Ann loved it there because Ricky could run free. They always had a grand time, but all vacations must come to an end, and now they were packing the car to go home. Auntie Ann called for Ricky to get into the car. Auntie Ann's mother told her to get into the car.

"'But . . .'" started Auntie Ann.

"'But *nothing*. Get into the car *now*,'" her mother said, pointing to the open door and staring at Auntie Ann. Confused and upset, Auntie Ann got into the car, and they drove away. Auntie Ann was sobbing. Auntie Ann's mother said, "Be quiet *now*. Stop that." And that is how they left Ricky behind. It would be sometime later that Auntie Ann would learn Ricky had been shot on purpose. He was dead.

"After she calmed down from her encounter with the awful man on the telephone about King, and remembering Ricky's plight, Auntie Ann began to think about what to do now. She had to get him out of the house. So, she called the vet's office where she took King for vet care and asked about long-term boarding.

"A plan came into reality. She would board King at the vet's office. She would leave work, go to a nearby shopping mall, change clothes, go pick up King, take him to the mall, work him for an hour on obedience, take him back to the vet's office, go back again to the mall, change back into her work clothes, and drive home. Unless asked, she would say nothing. If asked, she would tell the truth. No one was hurt. King was safe. He was 'gone' from the house and, therefore, not a problem. What could be wrong about that?

"About a year later, unfortunately, the vet called the house with a reminder to update King's annual vaccinations, and Auntie Ann's mother answered the phone. To say she was angry is an understatement. She was furious. She confronted Auntie Ann, who told her the entire truth. She said if Auntie Ann could afford to keep the dog at the vet's office, then she could pay higher rent.

"Auntie Ann already paid rent to live there. Auntie Ann said to just tell her how much she wanted, and if she could afford it, she would pay it, but if she couldn't, then she would find someplace else to live that she could afford. She explained about the man on the phone and that she just could not give King up.

"Things were tense, but a few months later, it was Auntie Ann's wedding, and Auntie Ann went to live with Roger, her new husband, who was the man of her dreams, and they and King moved to the Air Force base. In fact, Auntie Ann and Uncle Roger's first baby, Auntie Marcia, learned to walk by hanging onto King, and they had several interesting adventures over the rest of his life."

Stories like this made me, Miste, feel safe. I knew I had a home for the rest of my life. I had a home I loved and a family who loved me.

CHAPTER 16

BEWARE OF THE PARK

Yesterday started out to be an exciting day. There were all sorts of activities in the front yard. Then, all sorts of people showed up there. It seemed to me there were new dogs arriving from all over the world. It was all very exciting. Another fun activity, and I was ready! Activity is my kind of fun!

It was supposed to be like a walk in the park. You were supposed to encounter things you might see along the way. Well, *every* park I have been in over here has been really fun. Auntie Ann and I started our walk, and I was happy that I wasn't even having to "heel." I could pull. *Whoopee!* We walked along, meeting people, and the wonderful bucket with the treats in it was there. That is where they rattle this bucket with loud metal stuff in it, and it is supposed to scare you, but there are really very good treats in there, and you run right up there and get them before another dog beats you to it—but someone forgot to put the treats in it. I suppose that should have been my first clue, but I know humans can be forgetful, so I didn't think anything about it. Then, suddenly, we heard gunshots. I jumped (who wouldn't in my paws?). I checked out Auntie Ann. She was okay; then I checked out the area but saw nothing, so we continued. There was the umbrella. The umbrella is supposed to be a sight test and pop out and scare you, but it doesn't scare me.

It popped out—no problem there—been there, done that, and then the plastic tarp on the grass and the wire thingy in the grass—for touch, to see if you are afraid of different surfaces and things that feel different on your feet—no problems there. I was thinking this must be an obstacle thing—maybe some kind of agility thing.

But then this weird man came stumbling out of this tepee thing. He was just curious to look at, but then he turned toward us and started yelling; then I realized this was a dog murderer! He was coming after *me*. No one is faster than a Border Collie, and I was out of there. I whizzed past Auntie Ann and was perfectly willing to take her with me, but she was gonna have to move! She didn't budge. I hit the end of the leash (I still have a sore neck), and I realized she wasn't moving; the guy was retreating, so I came back and barked at him to let him know he'd better keep going!

This other man and Auntie Ann were talking, saying I failed some sort of test. What test? Was I supposed to stand there and get murdered? Where was Crieff to protect us? Does everything have to be a test all the time? I thought this was supposed to be a nice walk in the park. Let me warn you, my friends—this was *not* a nice walk in the park.

Cowboy, my Australian Shepherd friend, "passed," and everyone was congratulating him. He even got to go to the party afterward.

I got left at home. Auntie Ann said she didn't want me any more upset than I already was. After my part of the test, I sat in the office and watched out the window. Doesn't that count for something?

Auntie Ann gave me hugs and said she didn't hold it against me for not "passing"; she said that I would never leave here and that I was in this family forever. I just guess I have a lot to learn. I do have a *lot* to learn if anyone expects *me* to stand out there, by myself, and not *run* when a dog murderer comes charging after *me*. I just don't understand why leaving him in the dust isn't the preferred action of choice.

Auntie Ann jokingly (well, I *think* it was jokingly) pointed out that *all* of the German Shepherd Dogs had passed this "test," and the one who failed was the Border Collie. Well, my answer to that is: "Then let the German Shepherds do the guarding; that's fine with me. I will herd the sheep." I know my family loves me regardless, because their hugs and kisses last night told me so, and when Auntie Ann was having charley horses in her legs because of the "test" (another reason for me to dislike this "test"), I was the first one there to console her and get her mind off the pain. Of course, Crieff was still out in the run, so he couldn't get to her side, but, consider this: I was the one smart enough to be in the right spot at the right time . . . so, *there*!

CHAPTER 17

LIFE AFTER THE TT

Take me, for example; I don't know how these people got along without me. Even if I didn't pass the ATTS test—that's the American Temperament Test Society test, I am still a guardian.

Take today, for instance. No one is here except Auntie Ann, Rayne, and me . . . well, and the boarding dogs and Crieff and Scotia, who are out in the run, and all the other Shepherds out there—Gerrie, Mindin, *et al.*

Anyway, there are no other humans here, so I have to be on guard duty. I have to watch the front driveway in case someone comes in there. Then I have to patrol the house to make sure everything is as it should be. Then I have to keep an eye on Auntie Ann to make sure she's okay, and, since she's upstairs, that means I have to constantly run up and down the stairs to check the front, patrol the house, and run upstairs to make sure she's okay. Remember,

I am the demo dog in the class, which means I have to show the new students how to do stuff, which is a lot of work.

When class is over, we come home, and Auntie Marcia comes home with us. She has her schoolwork. I think they call them "lesson plans." I usually take my break then and play with my toys. Finally, it is time, and Auntie Ann goes up to bed. I usually decline to go then, because I feel someone should be guarding Auntie Marcia. Besides, Auntie Marcia is sometimes so tired that she falls asleep in the chair! I worry myself sick about that. Sometimes, I just have to bark her to bed. It isn't pleasant, but you just have to put your paw down someplace and bark and bark until she wakes up, gets up, and goes to bed.

I, Miste, am the family guardian.

Speaking of guarding, Rayne has told us about Braveheart, who was really something. He was born not breathing, and Auntie Ann had to give him artificial mouth-to-mouth resuscitation for half an hour to get him to breathe on his own. Braveheart was premature. Most German Shepherd Dog puppies weigh a pound to a pound and a half. Braveheart weighed seven ounces. He fit entirely in the palm of Auntie Ann's hand. Some people called him the 'runt' of the litter. Auntie Ann hated that. Braveheart was so small he could not nurse off his mother because he could not fit the dinner buckets into his tiny mouth. So, Auntie Ann, Uncle Roger and Auntie Marcia had to hand raise him. When the puppies' mother was brought in to feed the puppies, they all ran to her except for Braveheart. He ran to Auntie Ann to get his special bottle. At first, he did not have the strength to eat from that either. Auntie Ann had to very, very slowly syringe the milk fortified mixture into his mouth every two hours until he grew strong enough to suck it from a bottle. Many people said Braveheart should be put down because he probably would be brain-damaged, but Auntie Ann, Auntie Marcia, and Uncle Roger stubbornly kept working with him.

After all that, Braveheart, as he was rightly named, turned out to be OFA Excellent, meaning his hips were the best - not common in German Shepherd Dogs. He also had excellent temperament and was a wonderful therapy dog. He was Auntie Ann's special dog.

Auntie Ann never worried when Braveheart was with her. She had no doubt whatsoever that he would protect her with all the force he had, which was very powerful.

Mo-X, a shuttle service to various airports, was in a large shopping center. Several years ago, a man was murdered (shot) in that parking lot. Often Uncle Roger did not come in until after midnight. It was very spooky in that parking lot. Auntie Ann used to drive there and park to pick Uncle Roger up from an out-of-town trip.

She would park there, kind of away from the rest of the cars, and then slide down in the seat, so no one could see her unless they came right up to the car. Braveheart had his radar on. He would quietly growl if someone was within one hundred yards of the car. If they came within fifty yards of the car, he would loudly growl and bark. If they got within ten yards, he would add snarling and hitting the windows with his teeth, barking, and growling. Nobody ever came over to the car to see if someone was in there or if there was something they might want to steal. He was quite effective.

Family protection has many faces. It was another hot day, and we all had to come inside to get the air-conditioning. We couldn't go anywhere in the car because it would be too hot—immediately—if we stopped someplace. So, we all settled in and asked Rayne to tell us another story. This day, she chose to tell us another story about King.

It was in Belleville, Illinois. Auntie Ann and Uncle Roger were moving from the Air Force base into a house on the outskirts of the city. Auntie Marcia was just about six months old. King, of course, was part of the family as well. The family didn't have much furniture or a lot of things. They lived in a two-bedroom apartment, so the movers were packed and ready to move by about 10 a.m. The moving men needed to get gas for their truck, eat lunch, and fill out some paperwork, so it was agreed that they would meet us at the new house at 2 p.m.

Two o'clock came. The Gafke family was there, working on last-minute preparations for the arrival of the movers, but the movers were not. They were not there at 3 p.m., either. At 4 p.m., Uncle Roger called the moving company's office, but they had already left for the day. Five, six, and seven all came and went—and, still, no movers came.

Finally, around 8 p.m., the moving truck rolled into the driveway, and three *very drunk* movers stumbled out of the truck and announced they were going to unload and leave the furniture and boxes—everything—in the front yard! It was going to rain that night. The front yard would not do!

A few years before Auntie Ann was married, she had had an incident. She was walking King in her neighborhood for the last time before bedtime. Four young men riding in a convertible with the top down saw her, but the streetlamp was out, and it was pretty dark, so they didn't see King, who was an almost-solid-black German Shepherd Dog with dark-red/tan markings on his legs. He blended into the shadows very well. The young men invited Auntie Ann to get into the car with them. She declined. They became more persuasive, and three of them got out of the car and started to surround her. Fear—real and total fear—rose up into Auntie Ann's heart.

King was silently and immediately at her side. He started snarling and showing them his gleaming white teeth. They had not been aware that the dog was even there. It all happened so fast. They piled over each other to get back into the car; King lunged out toward them and snarled the most dreadful sounds, snapping his teeth, fully ready to bite them. Auntie Ann was frozen in fear. After that, Auntie Ann decided she needed to be able to direct and control King to help out in a situation like that. So, she taught King that, when she took hold of his collar and said, "Easy, Big Boy," King should growl. If she patted him on the side, while still holding his collar, and said, "Easy, Big Boy" again, he was to growl and snarl even louder. She would continue this until he was lunging at the end of the leash.

Now, King and Auntie Ann played this as a game. He never bit anyone, nor was he even mad at anyone. It was a *game* to him. But being protective on the dark street was not a game—it was real. But Auntie Ann thought that, with this game, she could prevent a possible real attack and scare someone away before it got worse and the someone got bolder.

Now, here were these movers, determined to unload the furniture and everything out into the front yard. The management of this crew was not able to be contacted. Uncle Roger said to Auntie Ann, "Why don't you stand by the front door with King, so you can direct these men where to put these items as they come off the truck?" Auntie Ann moved to just inside the front door and sat King at her side. Uncle Roger went outside and into the yard to monitor the unloading and direct the men to the door. When the second man came through the door swearing and threatening, Auntie Ann slipped her hand into King's collar and said, "Easy, Big Boy." King growled.

The man jumped and yelled, "Hey! You hang onto that dog!"

Auntie Ann replied, "I've got him. You just put that box in that first bedroom."

The man muttered, but he put the box in the correct bedroom. That pattern continued. Auntie Ann told the men that, the sooner they got all the stuff into the correct places, the sooner they could leave. King enthusiastically played the "game." He had the hang of it now and threw himself into the role of *motivator*. When the men finished, they left. They were not quite as drunk when they left; all the furniture was in the house, and no one was caught in the storm.

I was impressed. I tell everyone in the household that, when there is some person we don't know or there is something else going on, I think everyone needs to check it out, but then I retire and let the German Shepherds take care of the problem, if there is one. They are bigger than I am.

CHAPTER 18

AMANDA'S TALENT SHOW

You would be right with your guess! I did such a wonderful job at Lauren's talent show that, naturally, when Amanda's talent show came up, guess who was chosen to be the talent? Yep! It was me.

We were to go for two performances. The first was tryouts. The teachers would watch the acts; since there were more acts than they had room for in the show, they picked the top ones. Then, if we were chosen for the show, we would have to, of course, do the show. So, Amanda signed up. We went into rehearsing. I had lots more lessons under my paws; I knew the girls better; I had the experience of the first talent show, and, I admit, I had a little more patience. So, we rehearsed our routine, and we went to the tryouts.

To get there, we had to go down some long hallways. There were doors on both sides of the halls, and I was sure these were classrooms. Schools are alive with bells. I had been doing "Reading to Rover" programs at lots of schools. We dogs, who had passed lots of very hard tests to be able to do this work, would sit out in the hall with our handler or owner, who had been trained and tested with us, and the children would come, one at a time, out to the hall to read to us. Usually, the teacher had a cute chair or rocking chair and a special rug out there to sit on and read. Then the short people would get a bookmark with my cute or funny picture on it, or, if they had read to one of my friends, with their picture on the bookmark. The kids collected the bookmarks.

So, when we were going down the hall and the bell rang, we thought nothing of it, but suddenly all those doors opened, and, all at once, more than a hundred kids flooded out into the hall, saw me, and flocked all over me. All Auntie Ann could see was my leash disappearing into the sea of short people. All I saw were all these hands outstretched, and I felt so many on me that I couldn't even count them all.

All my training and experience told me not to worry. Remember—when I first got here—how scared I was? Now, I knew they were not going to hurt me. I was okay, and so was Auntie Ann. We finally reached the gym, and Amanda was there. There were lots of short people wanting to meet me. I was happy to meet every one of them. I love short people.

All seemed to go well, except they cut us off before we were even halfway through our routine. Didn't they like us? People usually liked us a lot, and the other people there seemed to like us. Amanda seemed bewildered. I didn't feel like *I* had done anything wrong. We left.

Then, surprise! A few days later, Amanda got notice that we had been selected for the show, *and* we were the lead act. We were the show-openers! Did they like us? They loved us! I was walking on air.

Boy, oh, boy! Did we ever practice! On the day of the performance, Lauren came to help. We waited backstage. It was old hat now. I wasn't a bit worried. I was ready to make up extra tricks if needed.

The short people filed into the gym, and it filled up with several hundred of them. We were introduced, and the curtains swished open. The sound was deafening, hundreds of screaming short people. It took me aback, I will admit, but we were on a roll, and we needed to go forward.

The performance went very well. I threw in a couple of new things. I think I shook up Amanda a little, but she's smart; she picked up on it and made it look like part of the act. One time, I danced to the very edge of the stage, and the short people in the front row thought I was going to jump into their laps. Just a little thrill—*just kidding*. We spent the rest of the show in a special area where the performers were to sit, and I had young hands all over me. It was fabulous. It was delicious, too, as they all gave me chicken strips from Amanda's treat pouch.

CHAPTER 19

MISTE HERE AND THERE

I sleep in lots of different places. I nap in front of the door, in front of the stairs, in doorways. I need to know if anyone in the house moves. Well, I'm not really asleep. I'm resting my eyes, but my brain is still working.

I also have a crate in the office where, sometimes, I need to go because someone is here, or everyone has to go where no dogs are allowed. Someday, that won't be the case. Someday, we dogs will be allowed everywhere (as long as we behave ourselves), just like other social progress. They can in Scotland, but America is so young they just haven't learned these things yet. That's why they need dog schools so badly. It's social progress, you know, and you know how that goes. Anyway, I have another crate at the foot of Uncle Roger's and Auntie's bed. I like to sleep there. It started out Braveheart's crate. Then it was Rayne's crate, but she can't climb the steps now, so, it has become my bed. I guess that makes me special too. It is so roomy and comfy. Usually, by the time I get there, I'm very tired. I love to sleep on my back with four feet in the air. Usually, my head is stretched out, upside down. They all laugh at me. I don't care. By the time I get to bed, I am so tired they can laugh all they want if they have the energy. I don't; I'm sleeping. I'm trying to convince Uncle Roger and Auntie Ann that I would fit on the bed, right in between them, but that is not working out just yet.

You already know I have discovered how magical water can be. My friend Maggie had introduced me to it at her house by chasing water out of a hose, but then, I discovered how much fun it is to stick your head down into the water and swish it around. You can also paw the water into splashing up on you, and that is great fun. I tried to get all four feet and my head into a bucket yesterday by standing on my head in the bucket, but that didn't work. Then, Auntie Ann bought me a large washtub that I could fit my whole self into; that was fun, but then I thought a swimming pool would let friends in it, too. Finally, I convinced Auntie Ann and Auntie Marcia to get me a kiddie swimming pool. Unfortunately, twenty minutes after I got into it for the first time, I got so carried away with playing, I accidentally poked holes in it, and it was beyond repair. They just don't make things as strong as they used to.

I have lots of toys. I love toys. I love and play with all my toys; however, I do get in mind a certain toy I want at a particular time. Everyone says I am like having a two-year-old child in the house. I don't understand that; maybe they can't count—because I am one year old, not two! I have three toy boxes. One is in the office, one is in the living room, and one is upstairs. If I can't find what I'm looking for in one place, I go to another and then another. I will find the toy I am hunting for eventually. Of course, it is always a relief to find what you're looking for. Auntie Ann says I need to learn to pick up my toys and put them back in the toy box. Boy, there is a lot to learn here.

Auntie Ann says I am the only dog she has ever had who needs to have a pacifier toy in the car with them. I guess the other dogs just haven't thought of that or haven't insisted on it. But that's not my fault! Their loss is my gain.

Yesterday, I cut a commercial. It was complex and interesting. We had backed into this one. The people making the commercial had seen me at class; they called and wanted me. I wasn't convinced I was the best choice for this assignment. After all, I had never done anything like this before, but the client gets what the client wants in these cases, so, somewhat reluctantly, I went along with it. My main concern was that they got what they were after. As it turned out, I was perfect for the job.

The commercial was for University of Missouri courses online. It will be shown nationwide. The storyline goes: A "student" has her computer and is lounging on her couch at home. Her loyal dog is lying on the couch with her and keeping her company while she is studying, with the dog's head resting on the "student's" leg. All of a sudden, the "professor" starts talking. The "student" is unaware of the professor's presence in the room; only the dog is able to see the professor. The student is hearing and seeing the professor through her computer only. The dog is startled and looks "wary and worried" as the professor talks. As the professor gives the lesson, the dog jumps off the couch and runs up the stairs. The dog is out of there! At the end, the dog peeks around the corner to see if that strange, unseen professor is gone!

The shoot was complicated and challenging. I had to show emotions. I had to be under total control, both on camera and off.

I had to adapt to changes in script and quickly learn new routines, which meant I was shown what to do only two times. That's it. I had to do very long and complicated *down/stays*, often staying in positions that were not usual *down/stays* or *sit/stays*. I had the scene clapper snapped as close as four inches from my face, and I could not move or flinch. I had to repeat everything over and over, one shot right after another, until they got the "look" they were after, or until the other actresses and I got the whole thing together exactly. Yet, they were in a hurry, too, and were expecting the dog to do it the same way every time. I was expected to be a professional who was able to punch in with instant compliance and complete flexibility.

I think I handled it like a trouper. I worked very hard. I had to run up and down those stairs about fifteen times and do it instantly—no horsing around. I had to come quickly back down and set up to do it again. Those crew members had to get this done. We were there from 9 a.m. until 5 p.m. I had to peek around the corner about thirty times in succession. The rest of the time, I had to lie quietly on a *down/stay* next to our chair. The script kept changing. They didn't have a problem with that. The client gets what the client wants, but it was challenging from my point of view! I had to know a much wider range of behaviors. Thank goodness I did! The behaviors were very different from what they had first told us, but I did them anyway. Yay!

I was certainly grateful for all the places we had performed. I was grateful that we had to do things exactly as we were told and that we follow explicit instructions. I looked at Auntie Marcia and Auntie Ann a couple of times, like, "Are you *sure?*" "Yes," they were sure. I was grateful for all the classwork and exposure we'd had. We used lots and lots of the stuff we do in class. I was glad for all the exercise I had herding those German Shepherd Dogs. I would need the stamina.

Who knows? Jack, the director and producer of the commercial, said he would like to come to the December show. Auntie Marcia and Auntie Ann assured him he would see lots of tricks and maybe get ideas for further work with a wide variety of dogs. So, practice away, my friends. Showbiz is just around the corner.

One of the things they stressed is that "acting" is not supposed to *look* like acting. It is supposed to look like normal life—natural. That's the hard part. Most of our obedience is too precise and rigid; it is necessarily that way because it teaches us to follow directions exactly, but in acting, you have to fit into the story smoothly. For example, I had to *down/stay* on a couch, sprawled over the actress's leg! I had to peek around the corner, looking apprehensive. The peeking was fun, but the apprehension was difficult. You try to do it—you'll see. Did you have to look up the word first? Then, did you do it without laughing? Now, try teaching your dog to do it! See what I mean?

People say I have a lot of expressions. They say I have a lot of communication with my eyes. If the camera crew got that, then that's what they were after. If they missed that, then they would have us do it again. We shall see what they come up with. They surely did the "takes" enough times. I hope they got it. I did it. They just had to capture it.

They said I was the first dog they had worked with. It was interesting to me that they expected more of me than they did of the human actresses. After all, I guess they thought I'm only a dog—right? Just wait! If they get a different dog, see what they can get. I could show no tiredness but always enthusiasm, always freshness, and always the exact emotion they wanted: apprehension, surprise, caution, worry, uncertainty, peace, relaxation, trust, confidence, or curiosity.

Then, when I was off camera but still on the set, I had to be laid back, totally calm, friendly—but not *too* friendly—and quiet, and I had to display impeccable manners. I had to obey instantly. Since I have been known to go on "strike" with a twinkle in my eye, I got my top array of treats: chicken livers fried in butter, McDonald's chicken nuggets, my favorite dog treats, a sort of beef-jerky stuff, string cheese, liver sausage, and several others I might like. I can be a very independent thinker, and I do go on strike. I will simply lie down and wait for them, the humans, to get their heads straight and give me consistent signals.

When it gets ridiculously bad, I demand an apology by refusing to work unless they apologize by giving me a raise in pay. But Wednesday, despite a tough previous week in which I did have to strike, I tried really, really hard and used all my patience and my brain to come through and work like a trouper. They say sometimes I have a little streak of rascally contrariness in me. I would hate to think they thought of me as a computer! I can compute; however, I am not a robot!

A couple weeks later, I was asked to do another commercial. This time it was for the vet school. I had to go to the University of Missouri College of Veterinary Medicine. That's where they teach their students to be doctors for dogs. I know that, when I was a little kid, I was scared and definitely did not like "the vet"—short for "veterinarian." A veterinarian is what a dog doctor is called; sometimes, we just call them "the vet." I know there are times dogs have to get those sticky things, called "shots," to keep us from getting really sick. And, if we get hurt, we need to go get treated by the vet. If we do get sick, we need to go to the vet to get medicine so that we can get better. So, I understand the importance of a veterinarian, but I still don't like being examined by the vet.

But it is fearful sitting in the waiting room. The smells are so different from any other place in the world. I can understand the importance of this place, but I still don't like going through the exam and possible treatment. In the end, here I am fighting an internal war. Although I am very uncomfortable and fearful here, today I am only an actress. I must keep reminding myself that today I am only an actress—no exams, no treatments. I am just an actress.

I would help that school, however, because now I understand that we dogs need veterinarians even if we do not like to "see" them for any kind of examination. So, there I was in the waiting room of the clinic, with smells of medicine reminding me I was only an actress today.

The "shoot" (showbiz talk for when you do the performance for the cameras) was at the clinic of College of Veterinary Medicine, or what they call the "Vet School" for short. That place is probably like all veterinary hospitals that you go to, although it is also a school. It has a check-in desk and a waiting room; then you go down the hall to the exam rooms. I could tell some of the dogs were as nervous as I am when I go to the vet. I felt sorry for them, but I didn't feel nervous that day. I knew I was not going to be examined; I could relax. For example, I noticed they had large bench seats that looked like they were leather-covered and padded—very comfortable. Dogs were allowed on the furniture here. Imagine that!

I had had all that experience in the first commercial I had cut for the Mizzou Online classes with the student on the couch and the professor that no one but me could see. I knew that, in my part, I had to be a perfect patient. I could do that because I was not scared because I was there as an actress, not a real patient. Also, I had had all my manners lessons. They started setting up in the hall. There were, of course, lots of bright lights to set up and lots of people rushing here and there. Plus, there were regular hospital patients and staff. The crew was rushing to set up the cameras and stage it. That means telling the actors exactly where to go and where to stop, how to handle the dog (that's me), which way I was to face, when I was supposed to sit, the look they wanted on my face, etc. I am good at looks. I can raise one eyebrow at a time or look fierce, pleading, or happy. People would pet me, and I was to look pleased to meet them but not get up or break my *sit/stay*. I had to look like I belonged to these people I had never seen before. I had to not look at my Auntie Ann or Auntie Marcia, but at the same time, I have to take directions from them.

So, we did it. Students gathered to watch. We did "lights, camera, action." We had to take only one part over. It wasn't anything to do with me. Everyone wanted to meet me, and, of course, I wanted to meet them, too. Everyone was pleased, and so was I. Pleased, but very tired.

CHAPTER 20

THERAPY DOGS

I had never heard about therapy dogs before I came here, but I sure have learned a lot since then! Therapy dogs do all sorts of different things. Some people think we just visit and get petted, but there is a whole lot more to it. I have just started my therapy work, but Rayne has told me about other events our German Shepherd family has had in therapy work.

She said that, one time, the Shepherds were visiting the hospital, and in the hallway was a boy about five years old, sitting in a wheelchair, obviously very unhappy and obviously in a bad mood. With him were his mother, a nurse, and a woman who, we found out later, was a physical therapist. The boy was not wanting to get out of the wheelchair and walk down the hall like the physical therapist and the mother wanted him to do. They were getting nowhere with this little, very stubborn, and determined boy. Auntie Marcia had her therapy dog, a German Shepherd Dog named "Keeps." She walked over to the group and said, "Excuse me. My German Shepherd (she gestured to Keeps) says she can beat you"—Auntie Marcia looked straight into the little boy's eyes—"in a race down this hall with her at a walk!" The little boy looked at Keeps for what seemed to be a very long time. Keeps yawned and lay down on the floor. It looked like she was smiling. Auntie Marcia leaned down, and Keeps licked her cheek. It looked like they were whispering together.

"No, she can't," said the boy. Auntie Marcia shrugged.

"She says she is definitely sure she can, even if she is in a slow walk. But if you want to try, we can line up right here."

The little boy straightened his mouth with determination. He answered. "I'm ready." He slid off the wheelchair, and Auntie Marcia lined up next to him. The physical therapist chimed in. "Would you like me to tell you, 'Ready, Set, Go'?" Everyone looked at the little boy. He was watching Keeps. He glanced at the therapist and said in a dismissive tone, "Okay." The therapist called out in a race-official tone, "Ready, Set, Go!"

The little boy started off moving as fast as he could. He had an obvious limp. You could tell he was in pain, but his concentration was on Keeps and moving forward to stay even with her or get ahead. Auntie Marcia's concentration was on Keeps, too. She was keeping Keeps at a walk, beside the boy, at a pace he could manage, and letting him keep just ahead of her most of the time but letting Keeps surge ahead once in a while to keep it "real" for the little boy. The therapist, the nurse, and the boy's mother were in the cheering section. The boy was clearly struggling, but he was so absorbed in winning this race that he didn't even notice it and was pushing himself as hard as he could down the hospital hallway and back.

At the end of the race, Auntie Marcia signaled Keeps to *slow down*, which she did, allowing the boy to pull ahead with a final burst of energy. A huge grin surged across his face as he was declared the winner. The physical therapist, the boy's mother, and the nurse all gave Auntie Marcia a silent *Thank you*.

Everyone wanted to pet Keeps. Auntie Marcia was congratulating the little boy, and so was Keeps. She had a grin on her face, her tail was wagging, and the little boy kept hugging her and telling her she just needed to practice!

Our family of German Shepherd Dogs also visited the VA Hospital. They were scheduled to give a drill-team performance outside on a lovely late-spring afternoon, in the parking lot. Patients were brought out in wheelchairs, all except one, who was brought out on a gurney. This patient had a history. He didn't talk to anyone unless he absolutely was forced to talk for some reason, and then it was tense, terse, and usually in an angry tone. He was sullen and angry. He had no arms and no legs. He spent most of his time facing the wall. He refused to participate in anything. However, when he heard about the dogs performing, he said he wanted to see them, so they wheeled him down on a gurney and outside to the performance. After the performance, we asked the man if he would like to meet one of the dogs up close and personal. Surprisingly, he said "Yes."

We put one of the little dogs up on his gurney. The dog started gently licking the patient's face. The man started laughing. He loved it. Some of the nurses were in tears, but all of them had smiles. This is what we do. We try to soften the harshness of life.

Rayne also told the story of our therapy-dog program at a hospital that took care of children with behavior problems. In our program!" with this hospital, we took 4-Hers[14] (ages 7 to 18) and their dogs into the hospital to work with young patients there. We therapy dogs love being a tool to help. The patients love us, and the hospital staff loves us. In this program, they used *our* program as a tool in their discipline program. If the young patients didn't behave, they could not participate in the dog program.

The program was conducted in the hospital gym, which was located in the basement of the hospital. We couldn't get all of our 4-Hers and their dogs in the elevator at once, so we had to take a few at a time, both when we arrived and when we left. During the sessions, the 4-Hers, their dogs, and the patients paired off. For the most part, the patients picked which dogs they wanted to work with that day. Everyone did a variety of exercises and games, depending on the lesson plans for that day. Games might include who could get their dog to sit first, the dog version of musical chairs, or canine tic-tac-toe. Some of the patients were afraid of dogs, so they were starting with small dogs and working up to bigger ones. The children loved all of this. They never wanted the sessions to end.

One day, there was a patient who was autistic. He had become very attached to one particular dog, a tiny Poodle named Pickles. We were ending the session, and the first round of 4-Hers and dogs had gone up in the elevators. A large, boisterous boy, who had been working with one of those dogs who had just left to go up in the elevators, was running around the gym, trying to get another dog to play with him. As he ran past our autistic boy, he grabbed the leash and pulled it out of the autistic boy's hand.

"*No!*" yelled the autistic boy as he struggled to get the leash back. The staff gasped. This boy had *never* spoken to anyone!

---

14 See Miste's Vocabluary Chapter 22

"*No!*" the boy yelled again! By now, all of us were involved in getting the dog's leash and control back to the autistic boy. The staff was at least partially in shock. They were complimenting the dogs, the 4-Hers, and the whole program. Therapy dogs had done what no one else had ever done for this boy.

Several years later, Auntie Ann was sick, and so Auntie Marcia had to go by herself to direct a drill-team performance at a church event. While they were there, a young man approached Auntie Marcia and asked her if she was "Ann," and Auntie Marcia said she wasn't but that she was her daughter. The young man explained that he had been in the program for youngsters at the hospital, and because of the dog program, he had graduated from that program and was now a successful business owner in town. He loved the dogs and said it was working with the dogs that had kept him in the program and encouraged him to finish it. It is stories like this that make us aware of the impact the dogs have on the people we try to help.

Then there was the time Auntie Ann and Braveheart were walking down the hospital hall to report for a therapy visit they were to make, when a woman stuck her head out the doorway of one of the hospital rooms. She took one look at us and exclaimed, "Oh, he loves dogs." A nurse popped out the same door and rushed up to Auntie Ann and Braveheart. "Please bring your dog in here," she said as she gestured toward the door, where the woman was still standing. They learned the young man in the bed was a 17-year-old who was one of four teenaged casualties in a car accident. He was in a coma. The other three teens had been killed. The teen's nurses felt he was close to the surface, but they just couldn't quite reach him. They asked Auntie Ann to line the dog up with the teen's bed. The nurse picked up the teen's hand and stroked the dog with it. His hands had been in clenched fists, which the nurses had not been able to even pry open. She very rhythmically stroked the dog with his clenched fist and rested on the fourth count: one slowly, two slowly, three slowly, and rest for four counts . . . then repeat. Keep it in rhythm. Auntie Ann and Braveheart did this for five minutes, keeping track of time by the nurse's watch.

Try standing still for five minutes by your watch. Go on; do it right now—and by your watch. See what I mean? Standing still for five minutes is v-e-r-y hard, and *you* have only two feet to control. We canines have four!

Anyway, the nurse repeated the procedure over and over. One, two, three, and rest. One, two, three, and rest—v-e-r-y s-l-o-w-l-y.

Wait! The resting hand slid open on the dog! Then, incredibly, the now-open hand slowly and unsteadily slid down the dog again (in an even-slower movement than the nurse had been doing) very unevenly, but it was moving under the teen's own power—not the nurse's guidance. All the humans in the room burst into tears. *We did that! We therapy dogs do things like that! Wow! I love my job!*

Rayne also said our dog school has a courthouse program, where we go into court with children when they have to testify. It seems we calm them down and give them courage. Rayne said one of our volunteers and her dog arrived at the courthouse one afternoon and heard a lot of yelling outside the courtroom. The adults were yelling angrily at each other. When they saw the dog arriving, they calmed down. The court officer quickly disappeared and brought another person back with him. It seemed like they were shocked and surprised to see the difference. It seemed like the adults didn't want to upset the dogs! They wanted to pet them instead! The authorities were delighted with this added value to the program.

We can help with physical therapy. For example, patients throw balls for us to retrieve. That is much more fun than throwing it to a person. They can brush us, too. That always feels so good to us. They can put us through hand signals or some of our tricks and have us retrieve for them. I do lots of these things. Well, I'm not so solid on retrieving yet. I'm working on it, but I *am* good at brushing. People comment all the time about how soft I am. I also know lots of tricks, *and* I'm very good at silent hand signals. I'm very good at pawtographing. I love to do that because I love short people. That's where we put our foot on an ink pad and then on the reader's book. Then, our handler writes our name, the date, and the event next to the paw print. Short people just love that.

Schools have told us that, when we come to their bookfairs, they sell a lot more books. The kids have to have read some of the book to the dog before the dog of their choice will pawtograph it—we stamp our paw print in their personal book. In our regular "Reading to Rover" sessions, of course, we give out our current bookmarks. Kids collect these. We also are used in classrooms for behavior modification. We did a presentation at the University of Missouri College of Education on "Lassie in the Classroom."

We have done "Reading to Rover" at Daniel Boone Regional Library, the largest library in the area, on a monthly basis for many years. Also, we perform for them once a year with our drill team.

We also do programs such as "Paws for Finals" at colleges and universities during finals week to reduce stress for students during finals. They have been very successful.

Before I came, Rayne said that the German Shepherd Dogs were involved in 4-H. The 4-Hers wrote what they did in a national report form. These were judged, and one 4-Her was chosen from each county to go on to state competition, and then the one chosen from that went on to regional (several states), and the regional winners competed for the top six in the nation. These six each received thousand-dollar scholarships and were declared national winners. Our club had five national winners. Auntie Ann said that was more than any other club in the whole country. No wonder I had to work so hard. The standards were sure high! I see now. *Smart* is *good*, but it is not going to win unless you use it to accomplish your goals.

We also have a drill-team performance in which we are choreographed to music. We perform for patients in hospitals, nursing homes, and schools, and for fundraisers for not-for-profit organizations like the Cancer Society, Head Start, the Humane Society, tragedy situations, churches, etc.

We set up a booth for the Pain Committee event at the hospital. Several people told Auntie Ann that I would never be a good therapy dog and that Border Collies are just not suitable for that kind of work. How wrong they were. The Pain Committee brought patients down to us and got a firsthand demonstration of what the dogs can do to lower blood pressure and heart rates. They were very impressed. We changed some minds. Our therapy work is so new that lots of people think we are untrained (*cute*, to be sure—but untrained) pets, who are prone to making huge disasters.

To get this therapy job, we have to pass lots of tests on our public behavior and our temperament. We have to have impeccable manners in public. We also have to put up with lots of stuff—like other dogs barking in our faces; people we don't know arguing around us; people yelling over us; walking on all sorts of different surfaces like wire, tarps, and slick floors; sudden loud noises; kids lying on top of us; people in weird clothes and masks; different kinds of traffic; swarms of people flooding over you all at once— just *all kinds* of stuff.

We have to have a bunch of baths. You'd better like taking baths, 'cause we get sometimes four or five baths a week, which, of course, include all the brushing (including teeth) and nail filing.

Where I came from, we took a bath by taking a swim in the River Tay. That usually happened when we were trying to get some not-too-bright sheep out of the river before they drowned themselves. Nails filed? Nope, no need. Teeth brushed—nope. No time—and no time to get brushed, either. As sheep dogs, we wore our *work* coats. Brushed and washed? Why? You just get dirty again, working in the mud and running through the brush.

As therapy dogs, we find ourselves in lots of different places. Rayne told me about the time Braveheart found himself in a hospital doing a television program, *Pepper and Friends,* when the head nurse of the Intensive Care Unit came up to Auntie Ann and asked her and Braveheart to come back and visit a young woman who had tried to commit suicide. Since coming to, after being unconscious, she had not spoken or shown any kind of emotion; the woman didn't say anything but never took her eyes off the dog. Her eyes softened and relaxed.

Braveheart was a big dog. Most people could reach him from a hospital bed if he was just standing on the floor. But Braveheart did know a command, "Paws up!" which meant to put his front paws gently up on the side of the bed, with his back feet still on the floor so that the patient could reach him better. At the very moment Auntie Ann issued the command, "Paws up!" there was a loud noise of someone dropping a tray of things right outside the open door to the room. Braveheart thought she had said, "Hup," which is his command to jump up on whatever is in front of him, which, in this case, was the bed! So, he did! Now he was straddled over the very shocked patient, who was now on her back, looking up at a smiling one-hundred-pound German Shepherd Dog who was about six inches away from her face!

There was about a five-second, shocked pause from everyone. Then the patient burst into tears, threw her arms around Braveheart's neck, and sobbed into his plush, freshly bathed coat. When Auntie Ann started to move to direct the big dog off the bed, the nurse shook her head not to do that. They let the young woman continue to vent her emotions into the great dog. At last, the sobbing subsided into broken-breath, whimpering, and shuddering. Braveheart lowered himself to the bed slowly and gently started licking the young woman's hand. All was good. The dam of emotion had burst and been drained. Braveheart had been successful. All was good.

We also teach training for service dogs—all kinds. For example, we had a woman with multiple sclerosis. She was using a motorized wheelchair. The problem was that, when she went to the store, she had her purchased items put in a basket on the back of her chair. As she was returning home, people would steal items out of her basket, even the wrapped ones. She had a little dog, part Chihuahua and part Shih Tzu. We taught this dog to ride in her lap and bark at whoever touched the basket or anything in it. Of course, that immediately drew everyone's attention to that action and announced it was wrong. It immediately cured the problem.

Another case we had was a woman who suffered from narcolepsy. She would fall asleep just standing and talking to someone. Of course, then she would fall down, which could cause her to hit her head or injure herself in some other way. She would also go to bed and not wake up when her alarm went off. We taught the dog to go everywhere with her. So, if she started to fall asleep, her dog would nudge her to keep her awake. Also, the dog learned to nudge her and wake her up when her alarm went off, the phone rang, someone was at the door, or a timer went off. We have worked with PTSD patients, paraplegics, even quadriplegics, people with blood-pressure issues, seizure issues, balance issues, etc.

We don't get paid in money; we do get paid in adventures, but the most satisfaction we get is from knowing we have helped someone. We also know we have helped other dogs. Dogs often get publicity for the *bad* things they do. Often, it is not their fault. Their humans have not educated them properly, and they don't know any better. We get to show the good and wonderful things dogs do. That is why we have to work so hard at doing things right. We have to learn to look for, think about, and follow through with the right action, not just slop something together.

CHAPTER 21

DECEMBER SHOW

The first weekend in December has, for more than thirty years, been the time we do the December show on Friday night, Saturday night, and Sunday afternoon.

I had heard about this show since I first got here. Rayne told me (of course), and then I heard about it in every class I took. The show is free; there is no charge. It is our gift to the community.

Yes, I have performed with the drill team, but it seems those were "road shows." Road shows are shorter, smaller, usually simpler, and with fewer people and dogs involved. Road shows are those performed in hospitals, schools, libraries, and other not-for-profit organizations; they are not performed in our training building. In addition, I'm told, road shows don't have the lighting effects, decorated set, more complicated drills, and a much larger cast.

The December show has evolved. According to Rayne, the first show had Auntie Ann standing out on the floor, counting the drills out loud, and directing the team to go from place to place. The costumes consisted of winter scarves and stocking caps on humans and winter scarves on dogs' necks. That was it.

Through the years, it has evolved into a wide variety of costumes for each number and each in-between act.[15] One year, Auntie Ann thought it might add interest if *she* also changed costumes to fit an upcoming number. She went all in for it and needed a place to change. The closet seemed like the best place for the couple of minutes it would take. She practiced the change, and it worked and had the effect she wanted. The plan worked well on Friday and Saturday.

The Sunday show was going well, too. The weather was unseasonably warm, and the sun was shining. The team, dressed and ready for the next piece (which was "Singin' in the Rain"), was outside, in back, lining up, and giving their dogs a break while the in-between was on the floor, and Auntie Ann was introducing the "Singin' in the Rain" piece. Auntie Ann had slipped into the closet to change costumes and was trying to emerge in her new costume to introduce "Singin' in the Rain," but she couldn't get the door open. She knocked on the door. Nothing. She knocked louder. Nothing. She pounded on the door. Nothing.

The music started for "Singin' in the Rain."

Auntie Marcia was backstage after coming off the floor after the in-between; she heard the music for "Singin' in the Rain" and saw the team outside. At the same instant, she heard Auntie Ann pounding on the closet door and saw the jumps and some other props blocking the door. She ran to the back door and spoke very loudly: "They are singing about rain in here"; then she rushed to

---

15 See Miste's Vocabulary Chapter 22

the door and started tearing the props and jumps from blocking the door! The team became acutely aware that their music was playing and that they should be on the floor by now, and they rushed to "stroll" in. Meanwhile, there was a rush to unblock the closet door. By the first chorus, the team was on the floor and in the right time to the music to finish the piece! That was the last time Auntie Ann ever tried to change costumes in the middle of a show!

Rayne says you never know what is going to happen at the December show. Another year, we had a piece about the "Night Before Christmas," and we had a rollaway bed as a prop in front of a fireplace. In removing it, after the piece had ended, one of our performers, Jessica, got a finger caught taking the bed off the floor, and Jessica's finger broke. She finished the show anyway. What a trouper!

Another year, it snowed about eight inches two days before opening night. It was the only year we had to cancel the show. Somehow, Rayne said, we pulled enough people together to do it the next weekend. It was a little different and rearranged, but the show went on.

Another year, we had this Great Dane in the show. In the piece after his, imagine how surprised Auntie Ann was when she discovered this *huge* pile of poop in the middle of a main line of travel for the next piece, which was in very, very dim light. She quickly whispered, "Watch your step" down the line. Not one dog or person stepped in it, but there sure was a lot of whispering in the audience as they realized what was happening!

This was my first year in the show. I had heard of it, but had no idea of how complicated it was. It is a little like a whole different world. Rayne told me we had been working on our December show since the previous show ended. Our human crew packed up the decorations, costumes, and props from the show and cleaned the building again. In January, we have several people who choreograph drills for us: Whitney, Robin, Elizabeth, Camryn, Kassidy, Nell, Shay, Auntie Marcia, and Auntie Ann. Rayne said we start in January working on new drills and practicing our road-show drills. We get new members who have to learn both the new drills and the road-show drills. In addition, we have a pretty heavy on-the-road schedule in the spring and summer. We must prepare for all of those.

Rayne said our deadlines for the December show started in July. Folks had to be signed up for the show by then, making the commitment to attend practices and do the show. There are also deadlines for the final drills; music for the show drills must be turned in. There are also deadlines for in-betweens; signups for each drill are made, costumes are set, lighting effects are decided—stuff like that. I remember our crew starts deep cleaning in August, oiling the doors so they slide smoothly, checking out the lights, fixing things, and storing equipment we wouldn't need until after the show. A lot of the equipment is needed for classes, so it couldn't be stored until classes ended at the end of October.

Our crew must clean everything thoroughly. Our crew does a lot of cleaning; I don't have to do any of the cleaning, but while the crew is cleaning, I have to do *stand/stays* for costume fittings. We try on different costumes for different drills to figure out what we are going to wear in which drills. We also have to practice and learn drills and all the other stuff canine cast members have to learn. Our human crew has to clean the building from top to bottom at least three times, besides all the other stuff they have to do, as well as smaller cleanings like washing the floor after practices. Then there are the windows, which have to be blocked out, because how can you do drills in the dark if sunlight is pouring in through the windows?

We dogs have to learn to be very quiet backstage and onstage, too, but even when we are not in drills onstage, we have to keep our minds on the show and be thinking ahead to what comes next, and we must do it quietly. We can't play with each other or bug each other, and we must immediately obey our handlers at all times. It is exhausting work.

Then there are the things we have to get used to. We have costumes: hats, ruffles, different lights (mirrored balls, disco lights, black lights, rheostat coach lamps, strobe lights, net lights, lighted collars on us), and, sometimes, we're totally in the dark, with only the lights on our collars. Then there are the balloons, feathers, all kinds of harnesses and collars, boots, and coats (and who knows what on the coats) on us.

Then there is the dry-ice fog that rolls over the floor and sometimes covers you clear up; you can't see your feet, and you can't see your teammates next to you. The fog moves, too, and, at first, it's scary. You have to get used to it, because when you start disappearing and you can't see yourself, it's a l-i-t-t-l-e bit startling. The fog is spooky stuff, especially when it moves and swirls, and we always use a lot of it. Wearing helium balloons takes some getting used to.

We have a technician for music, a committee for props, a crew for lighting, a committee for decorations, a seating-reservation maker, and a parking crew.

The seating for the show is a whole new, tough problem on its own. Rayne told me we have had to go to reserved seating, because, otherwise, we have so many that, even with standing room only, we have to turn people away. The show is free, but you must reserve a seat. Another problem is that the show starts at seven p.m. on Friday and Saturday and at two p.m. on Sunday. People were showing up at five p.m. on Friday and Saturday, or noon on Sunday, to get a seat, bringing their children and their dinner. Food was getting dropped and smushed all over, and the kids were playing on the set and taking it apart. They were also damaging the decorated carts to the point where they couldn't be repaired in time for the show. So, we started requiring people to reserve seats, and we locked the building until we could have someone there to supervise.

Drill-team members have to be at the building forty-five minutes before the show, but Auntie Ann likes to get there about an hour before the show just to make a final check on everything. So, Friday night—opening night—Auntie Ann and I arrived at the building and opened the door. There, we saw little blue-star lights cascading across the ceiling among more than four hundred sparkling stars, with snowflake garlands reflecting the lights from the snowflakes and stars. The magical Christmas set, with its snowy scene, Christmas trees, wrapped packages, stuffed animals, green boughs, snow, glitter, and tinsel all lay in wait for the opening night of our holiday show of choreographed, costumed dogs and handlers dancing to fun music.

Josephine, a darling and many-time grandmother, and Shadow, her Standard Schnauzer, were dancing alone on the floor. Josephine was lost in her own thoughts. It was perfect as she and Shadow danced to dreamy music in the soft glow of the glittery "sky" and the multi-color tree and ring-gate lights. They didn't even notice Auntie Ann and me coming in. Auntie Ann said she felt all fuzzy and warm inside. This was exactly one of the reasons she put so much effort into the show—*the magic of it all.*

As I said, drill-team members had to be there forty-five minutes before the show to get unloaded and set up, just in case something unexpected happened, and we had to replace someone or rewrite part of the show. We canines had to have our different costumes in order (there are only about two minutes between drills), get used to the audience and the nervousness of our handlers, and, well—maybe our own four-footers' nervousness, too!

But right now, I was scared to death. This was my first show. I had worked all year on my moves, tricks, and commands. I had been bathed every day all this past week; my nails were perfectly filed, and my coat was shiny and perfectly brushed. Even the insides of my ears were cleaned, and my teeth were tartar-scraped and brushed. I was out to potty seven times before the show. When we went out to warm up, I saw all the people, and they were all smiling and delighted to see us. I felt good and maybe just a *tiny bit* more relaxed—just a *really tiny bit*.

Now, many people think of dog crates as cages and that they are, therefore, cruel. Nothing could be further from the truth. Our crates are our private bedrooms. We feel safe there. See, you might think we are getting closed in, but did you ever think we like the door shut because everyone else is locked out? We are safe and comfortable there. We get treats, food, water, and toys there. Sure, there may be times when I would rather be in the thick of things. But frankly, there are so many more times when the rest in my crate is very welcome. This was one of those times. Auntie Ann put me in my crate, and my whole body relaxed. I could get my bearings and get my paws under me. I was safe. I could sort things out.

Fifteen minutes before the show started, we made announcements to the audience: Any empty chairs can now be filled. There are to be no flash cameras (they blind us, we trip, and we miss our cues) and when the bathroom is open and when it is closed—announcements like that.

Also, the wagon people come out onto the set to hitch up. Wagons are the first drill in the show, because we can get hitched up before the show starts and unhitched during the in-between acts which follow. The in-betweens are very short vignettes put in-between the major pieces to allow folks to change into their next costumes and get lined up for the next piece.

The show flew by. It took everything I had to keep focused on what came next: changing costumes and rushing to get lined up in time for the next drill. I was exhausted at the end of the show. Saturday night was much easier. I had learned a lot on Friday night, and I wasn't so scared. The audience on Friday loved us. On Saturday, the show flew by. We are used to it now.

Sunday's show was in the afternoon, so there was a much shorter time between shows. I knew what to do so well that I could do it in my sleep. The show was so much fun. The audience loved everything we did. They loved our tricks, dance moves, unison moves, scent discrimination, set talks, advanced training, jumps, tunneling, and on and on. Some people have come to the show for years. One man came up after the show, when Auntie Ann invites the audience to come onto the floor and meet the dogs up close. He told Auntie Ann he had a terrible headache when he arrived, but now, after the show, it was gone. He loved the show. Another man came up and said he was the owner of the company that had built the training building in which we had just finished our show. He said, with a smile on his face, that no one had *ever* done what we had done with one of his buildings. His eyes drifted over the twinkling lights and sparkling stars and all the other lights.

Auntie Ann remembered when all the light wires and plugs were put in. Auntie Ann had wanted electrical outlets on every post on every wall. She wanted four tiers of overhead lights, and she wanted more lights in the closet and bathroom. The electrician argued with her, saying she did not want that at all. He said she needed only one outlet on each of the four walls of the building and only one-fourth of the overhead lights. But Auntie Ann insisted she wanted enough electricity coming into the building to handle the flow when maximum lights were on all of them. One of our Building Members who was an electrical engineer by profession once told Auntie Ann what she really needed was a nuclear power plant in back of the building.

When the show was over, we were all very happy with our performance, and we were all very tired. After Sunday's show, we have a cast party. The humans relax, eat, talk about everything and anything they want, and play games. We canines are so tired by then that we get some extra good treats, snuggle in, and fall asleep in our crates. The happy human chatter lulls us into happy dreamlands. During the show, we have to concentrate so hard, but, after, the pressure is off. We are clean, sleeping on our cushy cushions, warm, and so happy. Our humans are happy, and so are we.

I thought about the show and how many people of all ages loved it. I thought about the other performances we had done in other places; we have performed for some people who really needed us and were so grateful for us that they had pictures of us on their nightstands.

I am a therapy dog. I had worked and passed all sorts of tests, too. I had come from a barn on the side of a hill in Scotland, from parents and, in fact, from generations of those who herded sheep.

Now here I was, halfway around the world across the pond (ocean). I don't herd sheep. I've gone from sheep to show business!

As my exhausted eyes closed to nap, I wondered what my next year in America would hold. I had a family to serve and an occupation that kept me very busy and made me feel very needed—and which I love. Tomorrow . . . We will see about all that tomorrow . . . zzzz.

CHAPTER 22

MISTE'S VOCABULARY

A

Agility—A dog sport featuring how quickly a dog can complete a prescribed course over different obstacles like an A-frame, jumps, teeter-totter, sway bridge, swing plank, through tunnels, bar jumps, tire jumps, broad jumps, window jumps, and weave poles.

Alert—When a dog who is trained to detect drugs or other substances indicates to its handler that the dog has detected the substances in a certain place or on a certain person. Most of the time, the "signal" is very subtle.

B

Bitch—The formal name for a female dog, wolf, fox, etc.

Blood Draw—A veterinarian draws blood from an animal to test it for any kind of disease or deficiency.

C

Companion Dog (CD) is an important first step in dog-obedience competition. It involves dogs being able to heel on-leash and off-leash and stand for exam off-leash, to come when called off-leash and do *sit/stays* and *down/stays*.

Companion Dog Excellent (CDX)—A step higher than CD in dog-obedience competition, where the dog gets into *all* off-leash work, drop on recall, retrieve on the flat, retrieve over a high jump, etc.

CGC—Canine Good Citizen. There are ten parts to the test for this American Kennel Club designation. The test demonstrates the dog's ability to behave in public situations with the dog's handler.

Champion—You can show a dog in many parts of the sport of dog showing—conformation, obedience, agility, freestyle, treibball[16], herding, hunting, tracking, carting, dock diving, tricks, etc. Each sport has its own set of titles you may earn. Conformation is judged on a dog's physical build against a written standard for that breed. The dog that most closely fits the standard is the winner. That individual is awarded championship points (one or two for a small show, or three to five for a large show). When fifteen points have been won, including two majors (three points or more) under at least two different judges, the dog becomes a champion. All judging is on the dog's physical structure, movement, and temperament.

---

16 See Miste's Vocabulary—Chapter 22

Crate—A container for dogs. There are many kinds of crates— wire, plastic, wood, fabric, and metal ones. Some people think they are cruel and call them "cages." Perhaps there *are* people who use them that way on dogs, but, used properly, the crate becomes the dog's bedroom. It becomes a protected place, where a dog can relax with good treats, a cool drink, a warm cozy blanket in the winter, a cool haven in the summer. When traveling, crates are a welcome bit of home and a place of safety. Dog people refer to them as "crates." Dogs love them.

D

Drug Detection—Detection of illegal drugs and other substances. Dogs have amazing noses. Many dogs work with their law-enforcement partners to find those substances either in certain spots or on a specific person and alert their handler to the presence of them.

F

First Footer—The "First Footer" is the first person visiting your house when the new year begins. "First Footers" are considered as bringing you luck. They usually bring a small gift, usually a piece of coal. The host usually offers fruitcake, shortcake, or black-bun dessert for guests, and everyone sings "Auld Lang Syne."

Freestyle—Choreographing dogs to do tricks and dance moves to music.

4-H—Is a young people's organization for boys and girls ages 8 to 18. They are able to choose and take projects such as dog care, photography, outdoorsmen, knitting, sewing, several levels of foods, woodworking, cake decorating, horsemanship, livestock care and many more. 4-H has summer camps, demonstration days where members must present a formal demonstration of something to the group. Members fill out annual report forms that describe their work in their project. The reports are judged first at a local county level, then at a state level, then at a regional level, and then the top six are named national winners and win scholarships. 4-H works with land-grant universities and extension services.

Strawn-O-Lite dog care project, Columbia, Missouri, with project leader Ann Gafke met once a week for two hours plus many special events. Youngsters learned dog care, training, about dog showing sports and how they work, about dog breeds with their specific purposes, structure, identification and more.

G

German Shepherd Dog—This breed is one of about 12 that officially have "Dog" in the official name of the breed. Without the "Dog" the title "German Shepherd" would refer to the German caregiver for the livestock. Another example: Australian Cattle Dog. Without the "Dog" Australian Cattle would refer to the livestock.

H

Heel—An obedience term for the dog to walk within six inches of the handler's left leg and sit automatically parallel to the handler's left foot when the handler stops.

I

An **"In-Between"** is a piece put between two acts that are longer and usually have more participants in them. They serve several purposes. One is that they eliminate dead air while the actors are lining up, changing costumes, etc. backstage. They are generally no more than two minutes long. They contain a variety of content—like special skills that are not covered in the regular drill pieces or information about the set or the dogs.

L

Line—Every dog has a family, and every dog family is different. Some families are not traceable. You don't know, in some cases, who the dogs' parents are, let alone any grandparents or great grandparents. Then, there are purebred dogs whose ancestry can be traced but the dogs in it have been put together haphazardly. However, some people choose the dogs they breed very carefully for certain good characteristics like intelligence, temperament, physical soundness, OFA hips and elbows, abilities like herding stock, movement, or other characteristics. Those characteristics have been present in enough dogs, parents, grandparents, great grandparents, etc. that they are consistently reproducing themselves. These animals become a 'line' when bred properly, consistently reproducing themselves.

Litter Brother or Sister—Puppies born at the same time in the same group from the same parents are litter mates and are litter brothers and sisters. Puppies born in previous litters or successive litters are brothers or sisters or full brothers or sisters, but not litter brothers or sisters.

N

"Nay" is a Scottish word for "not."

O

Obedience—The word has two meanings. As a general term, it describes the dog doing what the dog's handler wants it to do in daily activities. As a dog-performance sport, "obedience" tests how well the dog follows directions in increasingly difficult levels in on-leash and off-leash exercises. These exercises are judged against a standard, and points are deducted for mistakes.

OFA—Orthopedic Foundation for Animals—"OFA" for short. The OFA reviews radiographs of a dog's hips and elbows for signs of hip or elbow dysplasia, a crippling disease of a dog's hip or elbow joints. Categories are Excellent, Good, Fair, Borderline, Mildly Dysplastic, Dysplastic, Very Dysplastic.

P

Pedigree—In purebred dogs, a written, recorded ancestry or line of descent, usually with each ancestor's titles and OFA status. A person can learn a lot about what is behind each dog and what strengths and weaknesses the dog has. Major kennel clubs maintain the ancestry records. In the United States, the American Kennel Club and the United Kennel Club maintain pedigree records. In the United Kingdom, this responsibility rests with The Kennel Club. Some breeds have additional registries of their own.

R

Register of Merit—The Register of Merit (ROM) is based on what a dog or bitch (proper term for a female dog) produces in offspring and what the offspring accomplish. To achieve ROM, a female must produce two champions and two major point-winning offspring.

Males must produce five champions and five major point-winning offspring. National breed clubs maintain these records for specific breeds.

S

Scrum—A term used in the sport of rugby and to describe disorganized groups of dogs at play.

Seeing Eye—The Seeing Eye is an organization in New Jersey that trains and places guide dogs for people who are blind.

Service Dogs—Service dogs are used to help one specific person. They are used for a variety of needs, such as picking up things from the floor for their person, balance assistance for their person to get up or walk, predicting seizures, hearing assistance, etc. They differ from therapy dogs in that they assist and watch only one person—their handler—as opposed to therapy dogs, who visit and help people other than their handler.

T

Tattoo—Edinburgh Military Tattoo is a famous extravaganza held through the month of August on the esplanade of Edinburgh Castle in Scotland. The Tattoo has participating groups from all over the world—bands, dance groups, military groups, native-culture groups, mounted groups, fireworks, and more than 100 bagpipers. It is always spectacular.

Therapy Dogs—Therapy Dogs work as a team with their handler to help other people. In contrast, Service Dogs are used in helping their person—one patient. Therapy Dogs help their handler to help many people, such as aides helping students read, helping children stay calm when testifying in court, cheering up people in nursing homes and hospitals, and de-stressing first responders and others in emergency situations.

Therapy Dogs International—An organization that sponsors national, standardized tests that have to be passed for certification as a Therapy Dog. TDI has rules to follow before, during, and after visits. There are several other therapy dog organizations. Many are listed with the American Kennel Club.

Treibball—PetWell Club describes Treibball as soccer for dogs. The objective is for the dog to push large inflatable balls into a designated goal.

Tunneling—Dogs going under and through the legs of other dogs, people, hoops, etc.

U

Undercover—Police and their canine partners often work undercover, meaning they do not dress as police officers but "go plainclothes," under a different, assumed identity.

Underworld Contract—The underworld refers to the world of organized criminal groups. When a person—in this case, a dog—has such great success in solving crimes, the underworld will "put out a contract" on that person or dog. That means the criminals will pay a lot of money to the person who kills that dog or person.

W

Whelp—"Whelp," "Whelped," and "Whelping" are terms meaning "giving birth to." Also, "a whelp" is a newborn puppy. "A mother dog whelped a litter in the Kansas City Depot" means she gave birth to her puppies in the Kansas City Depot.

ABOUT THE AUTHOR

Ann Gafke grew up with dogs and has been training dogs for 60 years—for most of that time, helping others train their dogs. The stories in Miste's book are drawn from these experiences.

Her 4-H dog care program produced five national dog-care scholarship winners. The work of her students has been published by National Geographic in the book *Dogs on Duty* and in the book *Pets and the Elderly*. Missouri mental-health organizations honored her therapy work.

The American Kennel Club used her German Shepherd Dogs in its educational slide show on the German Shepherd Dog standard to represent ideal Shepherd temperament. Her dog, Yana, because of the champions she produced, and her own championship, earned membership in the Parade of German Shepherd Dog Greats.

Ann graduated from the Missouri School of Journalism with membership in the Alpha Phi Fraternity and Theta Sigma Phi, now the Association for Women in Communications. She became the first woman member of AFTRA (American Federation of Television and Radio Artists) as on-air talent in a television newsroom in Kansas City.

After three years, she moved from television news to dog training when she decided to be a stay-at-home mom to raise her children herself, feeling she would do a better job of than someone else might. Her dog training began as an informal service in the yard of Air Force Base housing where she lived with her husband, Roger. Her training became more organized when she and Roger moved to Columbia, Missouri, in the late '60s. It was first delivered on parking lots in downtown Columbia and then in her own training building in the early '90s. She applied the story-telling journalism experience into her dog training—creating a six-day-a-week dog school, dog-drill team, and 50-plus member therapy-dog unit serving Central Missouri.

In her dog school, Ann has mirrored balls, disco lights, strobe lights, black lights and bubble machines in the ceiling and decorated walls featuring Drill Team canine members.

Throughout the year, the Drill Team and Therapy Dog teams have scores of performances and therapy visits for schools, hospitals, libraries, nursing homes, and non-profit organizations, and accompany children in court to testify, helping the children keep calm in the traumatic situation.

Some of her dogs have been in plays, movies, and Hallmark-card shoots. They have been print models for Travis Duncan Photography. Their German Shepherd, Scarcity, had her own Christmas card, memo pad, mouse pad, and photo insert in a picture frame. Miste, their Border Collie from Scotland, starred in a nationwide commercial for Mizzou online classes. The commercial was aired during the Cotton Bowl.

Thank You

I offer a deep "Thank You" to the wonderful people who read drafts of Miste's book, offered suggestions and identified errors in the text.

They include: Elena De La Peña, Bob Dudley, Art Gafke, Lauren Gafke, Marcia Gafke, Roger Gafke, Lila Gracey, Brenda Hickman, Lynn Hill, Andrea Kaiser, Mary Newman, Chris Norton, Ruth O'Neill, Mary K. Romesburg, Ellen Wolfe, and the editorial staff of 1106 Design.